Paradise Restored

Sermons From Revelation
For Lent And Easter

Bill Mosley

CSS Publishing Company, Inc., Lima, Ohio

PARADISE RESTORED

Copyright © 2004 by
CSS Publishing Company, Inc.
Lima, Ohio

For more information about CSS Publishing Company resources, visit our website at www.csspub.com or e-mail us at custserv@csspub.com or call (800) 241-4056.

ISBN 0-7880-1992-9
PRINTED IN U.S.A.

To
Charles and Verlyn Mosley
and
Jeanne Weisbaker

Table Of Contents

Sermons On The Revelation Texts
In The Easter Season (Cycle C)

Preface

The year 2000 and the furor over the Y2K bug brought increased interest in the end of the world and the final judgment. Scary movies, television specials, books, and websites continued to grab for public attention. This fad merely takes advantage of a void in the public mind. General knowledge of what the Bible says has declined in recent years. But the fad also fosters the old idea of the God of Wrath who comes only to judge. These sermons lift up the book of Revelation, provide background for understanding it, create interest in further study of apocalyptic literature, and show its emphasis on the redemptive power of Christ.

John of Patmos wrote in a time of persecution and had to veil his message in coded language. Some of that code is lost to us. We preach to an audience used to media full of reruns, commercials, and recurring themes. Some of our hearers can recite verbatim the text of songs from the radio, commercials on television, and lines from movies, and many of these are from years ago. That knowledge comes from endless repetition — "saturation advertising," as it were. I have tried to use the technique of repetition in these sermons; major themes are repeated from sermon to sermon, and this madness has a method. Repetition can aid the memory. However, care should be taken that the preacher who uses this technique conveys the repeated material with freshness. You may think that recorded media such as television commercials have the unfair advantage of "canned freshness," but consider that the actors may have rehearsed and performed their lines many times in order to capture their spontaneity. We can learn from them.

Year C of the Revised Common Lectionary has six texts from Revelation in the Easter season. Combining the seven letters with the Easter texts ties the Lenten pilgrimage to the Easter celebration, just as John's vision moves from the practical consideration of conditions in the seven churches to the glorious sight of the

New Heaven and the New Earth. In both seasons, as in each of these sermons, the focus is on new life in Christ.

A seminary professor taught me to end every sermon with a prayer, and I have done that. One Sunday early on, I thought to use a prayer of Peter Marshall's. I liked it so much that I have kept the form of it and modified it every Sunday since then. I have lost the original and the source of it, but the formula has become a sort of "sign-off signature." It also serves to crystalize the point of the sermon in one or two sentences.

I have used many sources for the background and exposition in these sermons, and some of the sources are lost to me. Back in 1973, the American Lutheran Church Women devoted their monthly Bible Studies to Revelation, and I still have and use the resource developed for that study and published by Augsburg Publishing House: *Courage for Today — Hope for Tomorrow* by Esther Onstad. Arne Unhjem's *The Book of Revelation*, Lutheran Church Press, 1967, came to my attention at that time. I regularly consult *The Interpreter's Dictionary of the Bible* (Abingdon, 1962), and *The Interpreter's One-Volume Commentary on the Bible* (Abingdon, 1971), which were gifts from former congregations. Much of the history on the seven churches came from *Eerdmans Handbook to the Bible* (1973). More recently I have heard lectures by Dr. Timothy Lull and Dr. Barbara Rossing. I have also found many websites on the Internet to be very helpful.

I want to thank my friends on Ecunet, all my congregations in Texas, and CSS Publishing Company, publisher of *Emphasis, A Preaching Journal For The Parish Pastor.*

Revelation 2:1-7
Ash Wednesday

The Letter To Ephesus

In the season of Lent we prepare for Easter. The forty days before Easter are supposed to be devoted to purification of self, and meditation on the great sacrifice of Christ on the Cross of Good Friday. Most churches begin Lent on Ash Wednesday with the imposition of ashes. You get a black cross drawn on your forehead to remind you of the burnt offerings, of the giving up of life, that you are dust and to dust you shall return. By coming to the altar to have that cross put there, you are surrendering yourself to the discipline of the cross of Christ. It's like forty Good Fridays all concentrating on the cross.

So why are we looking at the book of Revelation this Lent? There's no great hymn to the emptying act of Jesus, such as in Philippians. There's no statement of making the crucified Christ a priority, as in the Corinthian letters. There's no theological homage to salvation by grace through faith in Christ Jesus, as in Romans. And there's no description of the Passion (or outpouring) of Jesus in the last week of his life, as there is in all four of the Gospels.

In fact, young Martin Luther objected to having Revelation in the Bible at all. It seemed to him to be missing the point of the cross but instead was given to triumphalism. He thought Revelation was a book of judgment instead of a book of grace. Young Luther thought that Revelation didn't serve the love of God for the world but instead fed the idea of a wrathful God who delighted in grotesque punishments.

Years later Luther changed his mind about Revelation. That picture from the young Luther is the one most people get when they don't really want to look at the real meaning of the book. And it is the deeper meanings to be found in the book of Revelation that we want to look for this Lenten Season.

The crucified Christ is there, in every verse of the last book of the Bible. The Christ we see in the vision of John is the Christ who became the sacrificial Lamb of God, who gave his life for the salvation of the world, who became the ONE who is worthy before God the Father, and it is because of the cross that God sends Jesus to judge. This Jesus is the Lord of the Church, the Lord of history, the Lord of the New Heaven and New Earth, and all creation gives him thanks and praise. This is the Lord of Lent.

And this is the way to understand this most difficult of New Testament books. There are bizarre visions here, and the devil appears several times in several different forms, but Jesus also appears many times in many different forms. John really believes that the world is in a tumultuous battle between good and evil, and that first appearances can be deceiving. He's warning us to look below the surface. To search for hidden meanings. And in Revelation's vision we find symbols and visions with varying degrees of meaning. Some have one meaning, some have several meanings, some have many meanings, and some have no apparent meaning.

Revelation begins with seven letters, one each to seven churches in Asia Minor. They seem to be churches that John is familiar with, and he knows their personalities and character. The churches are Ephesus, Smyrna, Pergamum, Thyatira, Sardis, Philadelphia, and Laodicea.

To understand these seven letters, we first have to set the stage for how John receives them. The Romans have put John on their prison island, Patmos. The Spirit calls John to write to seven churches. He couches his message in symbolic language, cradled in his vision of the risen Lord who transcends anything in human experience.

It's on the Lord's day that John has this vision. He hears a loud voice like a trumpet saying, "Write this vision and send it to the seven churches by name." He turns to see who is speaking, and sees a magnificent Jesus in a white robe amidst seven golden lampstands and holding seven stars. Jesus explains that the stars are the angels of the seven churches and the lampstands are the seven churches.

In the Sermon on the Mount, Jesus calls us to be the light of the world, a city set on a hill, a lampstand that is not hidden under a bushel. Here in Revelation, Jesus stands among the lampstands and he holds the angels of the churches in his hand.

See, the Christ of Revelation is past the crucifixion, but he is looking to encourage the church and Christians who are not past their own sacrifice and suffering. John writes his vision to encourage people who face the persecution of the last part of the first century.

John is writing to a church under persecution, probably that of the Emperor Domitian Caesar, who was assassinated in 97 A.D., so we are experiencing a message given around 95 or 96 A.D. John wants us to know that Christians who face the lions and the fires, whether they survive or not, will see paradise at the throne of God and the Lamb. They won't hunger or thirst, they'll have springs of living water, and God will wipe away every tear. Not that they won't have tears, but that they will be comforted.

The first letter is to the church at Ephesus. Now that name should ring a bell in your memory. It certainly would to every Christian in the first century who heard or read this book. Ephesus had a famous church, even then. Paul lived and worked there three years. It was where Paul's letters were first collected, and several people of the New Testament were from there.

In the dictation to John of Patmos, the Lord says this church is pure, but unproductive. They believe but produce no fruit.

He says basically three things to this church at Ephesus.

1. He commends them for their patient endurance. This is a main theme of Revelation. Patient endurance is the Number One virtue in Revelation and is always rewarded. It's even mentioned twice in this very short letter. This church has not grown weary, so it is still living and breathing as a church.

A church tends to have a personality. It gets into habits, maybe even ruts. Lyle Schaller, a consultant on church administration, says a church does what it has the most practice doing. Ephesus has endurance.

2. Secondly, the letter says the church at Ephesus has tested those who call themselves apostles, but are not, and found them to be false. Testing is a theme elsewhere in the Bible. Test the spirits, James says. I think Ephesus must have tested everybody. You have

to test the whole bunch to separate out the good from the bad. And testing is no good without rejecting the bad. Why do it just for the fun of it?

I used to work with vinyl siding. On one job we used tan colored siding. It comes in 10-foot long boxes with 24 sheets or panels in each box. The first box had two panels that weren't the right kind. They were made of the same stuff, the same size, the same color, but we couldn't use them. They were a different style. They didn't pass the test. Whoever packed the boxes for shipping made a mistake. Now here's an interesting point: If we had gotten these out first, we wouldn't have been able to tell they were wrong until we came to the right ones. We had to have the right ones to compare. I put the wrong kind in an empty box and wrote on it: BAD.

This is one lesson we will meet again in Revelation: testing, looking to tell the difference between good and bad.

3. The church at Ephesus has endured patiently, has tested for false teachers, but they have abandoned the love and works they had at first. Maybe they hadn't practiced love and works sufficiently to make them a habit, part of their personality. The Lord says, "Repent and return to those good things you were doing." If they don't, the Lord will remove their lampstands.

For John of Patmos, the victory of the Lord at the end of time is sure and certain, and there is comfort for the believers, and uncounted multitudes will be saved, but for some, the lampstand will be removed. They could lose their church. They could lose their salvation. Is this good news? Can this be a message of grace? Well, no. But it is a warning of what happens when you lose the freshness of a faith that brims over with love, generosity, forgiveness, patience, open-handedness, serenity, and good works. Practice these gifts. Make them your habit. For the next forty days, do something every day that strengthens your faith, reinforces your habit.

Some people give up something for Lent. Why not instead, *add* something? An extra moment of prayer, a little time to read your Bible, maybe in the book of Revelation, or memorize a bit of scripture every day. It will add to your habit of faith, and give you tools for testing the spirits.

For this Lent, we have a vision of the Lord of the Church who knows our suffering because he has given his blood for us, and it is in his name that we have patient endurance, test all who come among us, and constantly renew our enthusiasm in faith.

Lord, help us to know the joy that is ours when we say no to everything that makes it more difficult to say yes to you.

The Letter To Smyrna

About 35 miles north of Ephesus is Smyrna. It's called Ismir, Turkey, today. In the first century it was already very old, was a commercial center, and had a temple to Emperor Tiberias. This temple made the city an important showcase for the state religion. Loyalty tests would be frequent and well publicized. We know of some very public examples of Christian executions at Smyrna. Probably the best documented of the ancient world was the death of Polycarp, Bishop of Smyrna, in 156 A.D. Polycarp was burned at the stake. The legend says that as a youth Polycarp was a disciple of John. He would surely have read Revelation and noted the letter to Smyrna. We know for certain Polycarp knew Ignatius of Antioch, who wrote seven letters we still have and himself was thrown to wild beasts in the arena at Rome. Polycarp also knew Irenaeus, who as a child heard Polycarp speak and himself was martyred in 202.

John of Patmos is writing to a church under persecution, probably that of the Emperor Domitian Caesar, who was assassinated in 97 A.D., so we are experiencing a message given around 95 or 96 A.D. John wants us to know that Christians who face the lions and the fires, whether they survive or not, will see paradise at the throne of God and the Lamb. They won't hunger or thirst, they'll have springs of living water, and God will wipe away every tear. Not that they won't have tears, but they will be comforted.

The Romans have put John on their prison island, Patmos. The Spirit calls John to write to the seven churches in Asia Minor which lie on a circular road, like the round trip an evangelist or missionary would make to end up near his home. He couches his message in symbolic language, cradled in his vision of the risen Lord who transcends anything in human experience.

It's on the Lord's day that John has this vision. He's probably thinking he would be in fellowship with other believers on this day. He longs to connect, to bridge the separation, but he's in prison. He hears a loud voice like a trumpet saying, "Write this vision and send it to the seven churches by name." He turns to see who is speaking, and sees a magnificent Jesus in a white robe amidst seven golden lampstands and holding seven stars. Jesus explains that the stars are the angels of the seven churches and the lampstands are the seven churches.

In the Sermon on the Mount, Jesus calls us to be the light of the world, a city set on a hill, a lampstand that is not hidden under a bushel. Here in Revelation, the Lord Christ stands among the lampstands and he holds the angels of the churches in his hand.

See, the Christ of Revelation is past the crucifixion, but he is looking to encourage the church and Christians who are not past their own sacrifice and suffering. John writes his vision to encourage people who face the persecution of the last part of the first century.

- Ephesus, the loveless church
- Smyrna, the persecuted church
- Pergamum, the compromising church
- Thyatira, the corrupting church
- Sardis, the dead church
- Philadelphia, the faithful church
- Laodicea, the lukewarm church

In the first letter, the Lord calls the church at Ephesus to task for being the fruit of shallow soil; they began with much love and great and good works, but they have lost their zeal. About the only thing in their favor is that they are pure. They test everyone and find out the false apostles and teachers.

The second letter, the one to the Smyrna church, is short and glowing in praise for the small church that bravely faces death, but warns of two things: the hypocrisy of those who say they are faithful but are not, and a coming time of tribulation that will last ten days.

It's difficult for us to understand this today. We have it too easy. We remember the '50s and '60s when it was the socially correct thing to belong to a church. Today, the rule we go by is politically correct. And it's not exactly politically correct to be Christian. But it still looks good to have on your resume that you belong to a church.

We don't have to watch our membership for infiltrators yet, but some are saying the day will come. In first century Smyrna, there were those who said they were Jews but in reality had evil in their hearts. See, in the Roman Empire, the worship of the Hebrew God was allowed. Jews were exempt from emperor worship. And for a few decades after the crucifixion, Christianity was considered an offshoot of Judaism. By the '60s when the Jews were about to revolt, the split between the church and synagogue was widening and about to get violent. So they couldn't trust each other. And even today it's normal to ask Jewish people if they practice their religion and which branch. Do they keep a kosher kitchen?

The slander in Smyrna was probably the passing of rumors that Christians were agitating against the government — an easy slander to pass off because the government was anti-Christian, while the church was not necessarily anti-government. Being loving, forgiving, and accepting, faithful Christians don't get a lot of practice defending themselves.

John is at great pains to point out that non-believers, even enemies of God, look just like true believers. Everything that glitters is not gold. And what sounds like truth may not be the truth. This is why gossip and rumors can be very dangerous.

The coming tribulation will last ten days, and this is just an expression for completion. We might say, "It's not over till it's over." Or even, "This too shall pass."

John's word of encouragement to Smyrna is, "Be faithful unto death and I will give you a crown of life."

Well, I'm not sure I would be encouraged by the message that I would have to face death. I ask myself, "What would I die for? What will I give my life for?" I know I say sometimes, "I'd give anything for a ..." and fill in that blank with some tool I need to make a job easier, or some money to get something I want, or some food that would taste good right then.

On the construction job I risked my life quite often — climbing a ladder or a scaffold. You risk your life every time you get into a car or get close to large animals. It's even a sign of manhood to show that you're willing to take such risks. But are these real? If you thought about it, would you be willing to die to get somewhere sooner? Or get this or that job done? What are you willing to die for?

A church tends to have a personality. It gets into habits, maybe even ruts. Lyle Schaller, a consultant on church administration, says a church does what it has the most practice doing. Ephesus has endurance. Smyrna has faith and courage in the face of persecution. Both endurance and faith against persecution take practice.

Faithful endurance is always rewarded in the visions of Revelation. To Smyrna, the Lord says, "I know of your poverty, but you are rich. Maybe you look small and poor to the world, but to the Lord, you have riches beyond anything visible. You have faithful endurance."

A faith to die for.

For John of Patmos, the victory of the Lord at the end of time is sure and certain, and there is comfort for the believers, and an uncounted multitude will be saved. He warns Ephesus that for some, the lampstand will be removed. You could lose your church. You could lose your salvation. But for Smyrna he has the promise of a short but complete tribulation, and a crown of life for the faithful.

Polycarp, Ignatius, Irenaus, John of Patmos all faced suffering for their faith. Clearly, being a Christian doesn't mean we won't have trials and tribulations. They will come. We can respond in two ways.

We can grow bitter and resentful. We can harbor feelings of regret and guilt, and decide never to move beyond our affliction and back into life. We can try to make those around us share our misery instead of trying to share their joys.

Or we can ask, "What good can come out of this? How can this illness, this tragedy, this pain, be used for good?" Not to deny the reality of the suffering, but to deny it its power — to deny that the tragedy must only be a tragedy. It can also be a fertile ground for growth, a springboard for something good.

For this Lent, we have a vision of the Lord of the Church who knows our suffering because he has given his blood for us, and it is in his name that we have patient endurance, test all who come among us, and constantly renew our enthusiasm in faith.

Lord, help us to know the faithful endurance that says no to everything that makes it more difficult to say yes to you.

The Letter To Pergamum

You remember the famous story of Balaam and his talking ass? Well, it's actually a story within a story within an epic. It's over in the Old Testament book of Numbers, starting in chapter 22. The nation of Israel is approaching the Promised Land. By the power of God, Moses has led the nation to conquer and dispossess several peoples, and the Israelites are poised to enter Moab and Midian.

You know how in a war movie, one minute you might be seeing the whole battle and the troop movements and you're thinking in vast terms of the sweep of history, when suddenly the focus centers on some little thing that's happening off to the side of the main battle? And maybe it's several scenes of comic relief and you get to wondering why are we seeing this, when the main action is raging on the battlefield?

Well, something like that happens in Numbers 22. We've been seeing Moses and the Israelites progress ever closer to the end of the forty years in the wilderness, making friends here, absorbing other tribes there, fighting and killing whole nations on the way. Suddenly we're off to the side in a little intrigue with the king of Moab named Balak. He's afraid of Israel, and he sees the power of their God and he hopes to enlist some divine power against them. So he sends for a Babylonian prophet named Balaam.

So we're talking about two Gentiles, two people outside of Israel's tabernacle: Balak, a king, and Balaam, a prophet. Balak asks Balaam to curse Israel so he can defeat them. Balaam has a word from God: Israel is blessed and that's all there is to it. So he puts Balak off. Balak offers Balaam a house filled with silver and gold. So while Balaam is coming to Balak, riding on his donkey, we have this small story within the story within the epic.

The angel of the Lord blocks the donkey three times. Balaam beats the donkey three times. On the third time, the Lord gives the donkey speech, and the donkey says, "Hey, I've been your donkey a long time and I've never done this and you've never done that. Don't you think you ought to find out why I can't go forward?"

Just then Balaam is allowed to see the angel and Balaam worships God and the angel says to go with Balak's men but only speak what God says to speak.

Well, he gives four oracles and all say that Israel will prosper and Moab will suffer. There's an argument involving Balak's refusal to pay for his prophecy because it didn't say what he wanted it to say. Balaam is allowed to go home. Balak gives up and there is no battle at that time.

Later we read that Balaam is killed after the battle with the Midianites as part of the reparations. Later references to Balaam blame him for advocating the sexual corruption of the nation with Moabite women, who lead the people to eat food which had been sacrificed to idols. So he has a reputation as a kind of Judas — leading the righteous people astray.

Balaam is also given as an example of a foreigner who testifies to the power of God. I think this is truer to his story. But because his prophecy prevents outright battle and allows the intermingling of the two cultures, he gets the blame for the corruption. And it's this blame that John of Patmos assesses against the church at Pergamum, 1,400 or so years later.

In the Sermon on the Mount, Jesus calls us to be the light of the world, a city set on a hill, a lampstand that is not hidden under a bushel. Here in Revelation, the Lord Christ stands among the lampstands and he holds the angels of the churches in his hand.

- Ephesus, the loveless church
- Smyrna, the persecuted church
- Pergamum, the compromising church
- Thyatira, the corrupting church
- Sardis, the dead church
- Philadelphia, the faithful church
- Laodicea, the lukewarm church

In the first letter, the Lord calls the church at Ephesus to task for being the fruit of shallow soil; they began with much love and great and good works, but they have lost their zeal. About the only thing in their favor is that they are pure. They test everyone and find out the false apostles and teachers.

The second letter to the Smyrna church is short and glowing in praise for the small church that bravely faces death.

But the church at Pergamum he criticizes for accepting the morality and practices of the culture around them. It's no accident that he mentions Balak and Balaam, which to Jews instantly calls up the impure mixing of the nation, adultery, and idol worship.

Even in Rome the temples were built with two fronts. You brought in your meat for sacrificing through the temple door, and the priest inspected the meat to be sure it was of the finest quality, and then took some of it to burn on the altar. The rest went out the back door, where there was a storefront, and that meat was sold to raise money for the temple.

Now the question for Christians was: Could you eat meat that had been part of pagan worship? For some, it was a tempest in a teapot: idols are not real, so the worship is not real, of no consequence. But for others, bending at all was to accept that idol worship was real. And to buy the meat was to support the temple worship. It was a big question, and Paul addresses it in 1 Corinthians. The answer he gives is: If what you do causes the weaker brethren to stumble, don't do it. Even if you know it is not evil, avoid the appearance of evil, because others may not be so discerning in their vision. The strong need to set examples for the weak.

John goes further. He is at great pains to point out that non-believers, even enemies of God, look just like true believers. All that glitters is not gold. And what sounds like truth may not be the truth. This is why gossip and rumors can be very dangerous, he tells the church at Smyrna. To Pergamum the Lord says, "I will make war on you with my two-edged sword."

Revelation deals with the broad sweep of the end of time, and never mentions the name of individuals, except here. Antipas, a faithful one, a witness, was martyred at Pergamum. Probably because he stood out as different from the culture around him. He was probably made an example to frighten and intimidate the Christians and keep them from standing for their beliefs. Apparently, it worked.

A sword divides; it cuts; it kills. The sword of the Word of God divides us from the rest of the world. We can't blend in; we have to be different. That's what it means to be the salt of the earth, a city set on a hill. The sword of the Word of God kills our old self and cuts us off from our earthly desires. The war rages on about us, but we are a scene apart, a story within a story within an epic, and what we do, who we are, makes us different from the world, still a part of it, but different from it.

A church tends to have a personality. Ephesus has endurance. Smyrna has faith and courage in the face of persecution. Pergamum has compromised itself with the society around it. You can't tell the Christians at Pergamum from the pagans. They need to break their habit and get out of their rut.

For John of Patmos, the victory of the Lord at the end of time is sure and certain, and there is comfort for the believers, and an uncounted multitude will be saved. He warns Ephesus that for some, the lampstand will be removed. They could lose their church. They could lose their salvation. For Smyrna he has the promise of a crown of life for the faithful. For Pergamum he promises the hidden manna and the new name on the white stone.

Lots of people say they are Christian, believers in Christ. But what they believe doesn't make a difference in their lives. They want to blend in, to live in the same kind of houses, drive the same car, dress the same way and be like the rest of the world. But Christians are not called to be like the rest of the world. You know the old question, "If you were arrested for being a Christian, would there be enough evidence to convict you?" Part of the evidence is to be different from the rest of the world.

For this Lent, we have a vision of the Lord of the Church who knows our suffering because he has given his blood for us, and it is in his name that we have patient endurance, test all who come among us, constantly renew our enthusiasm in faith, even to being different from the world around us.

Lord, help us to be different in a guile-less righteousness that says no to everything that makes it more difficult to say yes to you.

Revelation 2:18-29
Lent

The Letter To Thyatira

Kurt Vonnegut is a famous author of surreal novels. He was very popular among college students when I was on campus, and I guess he still is. There is a note going around on the Internet saying it is a commencement address that Kurt Vonnegut gave at MIT.

Part of it says:

Wear sunscreen. If I could offer you only one tip for the future, sunscreen would be it. The long-term benefits of sunscreen have been proved by scientists, whereas the rest of my advice has no basis more reliable than my own meandering experience. I will dispense this advice now.

Travel.

Accept certain inalienable truths: Prices will rise. Politicians will philander. You, too, will get old. And when you do, you'll fantasize that when you were young, prices were reasonable, politicians were noble, and children respected their elders.

Respect your elders.

Don't expect anyone else to support you. Maybe you have a trust fund. Maybe you'll have a wealthy spouse. But you never know when either one might run out.

Don't mess too much with your hair or by the time you're forty it will look 85.

Be careful whose advice you buy, but be patient with those who supply it. Advice is a form of nostalgia. Dispensing it is a way of fishing the past from the disposal, wiping it off, painting over the ugly parts, and recycling it for more than it's worth.

But trust me on the sunscreen.

The truth is, Kurt Vonnegut didn't give that speech. It was a Chicago *Tribune* newspaper column by Mary Schmich. It was on their web site in 1997 when it was published.

From the Philadelphia *Inquirer*, Wednesday, Aug. 3, 1997:

> *If you're a Kurt Vonnegut fan — or even if you're not — and plugged into cyberspace, you may have gotten e-mail ... described as a commencement address given by the writer to the graduates at MIT. It begins: "Ladies and gentlemen of the class of '97: Wear sunscreen. If I could offer you only one tip for the future, sunscreen would be it." What follows is both wise and funny. But it isn't Vonnegut. "Kurt didn't write it," Don Farber, the writer's lawyer and agent, told* The Inquirer. *The real author is Mary Schmich, a Chicago* Tribune *columnist who had nothing to do with its appearance in cyberspace under Vonnegut's name. "Whoever did this is a thief," Farber said. "They stole her work and Kurt's name." For the record, Farber said Vonnegut laughed when he read [it]. "He was quite gracious," [Schmich] said, but she added that the episode underscored for her the Internet's "scary" side.*

So it was a scam, like the letter campaign to the FCC about Madeline Murray O'Hair, and the cards for the little boy with cancer, and the mob ring that steals kidneys. The scary thing is people with the best of intentions can be drawn down the wrong paths for so many of the right reasons.

The Romans exiled John to their prison island, Patmos. The Spirit calls John to write to the seven churches in Asia Minor which lie on a circular road, like the round trip an evangelist or missionary would make to end up near his home. He couches his message in symbolic language, cradled in his vision of the risen Lord who transcends anything in human experience.

He has a vision of a magnificent Jesus in a white robe amidst seven golden lampstands and holding seven stars. Jesus explains that the stars are the angels of the seven churches and the lampstands are the seven churches.

In the Sermon on the Mount, Jesus calls us to be the light of the world, a city set on a hill, a lampstand that is not hidden under a bushel. Here in Revelation, the Lord Christ stands among the lampstands and he holds the angels of the churches in his hand.

- Ephesus, the loveless church
- Smyrna, the persecuted church
- Pergamum, the compromising church
- Thyatira, the corrupt church
- Sardis, the dead church
- Philadelphia, the faithful church
- Laodicea, the lukewarm church

In the first letter, the Lord calls the church at Ephesus to task for being the fruit of shallow soil; they began with much love and great and good works; now they have lost their zeal. But they test everyone and find out the false apostles and teachers.

The second letter to the Smyrna church is short and glowing in praise for the small church that bravely faces death.

The church at Pergamum he criticizes for accepting the immorality and practices of the culture around them. He tells them to avoid even the appearance of evil, because others may not be so discerning in their vision. The strong need to set an example for the weak.

And the church at Thyatira has a similar problem. Their strength is that they have grown in their good works. Love and faith and service and endurance have exceeded what they had at first. Remember Ephesus was just the opposite; they had started off with commendable good works but then had weakened. But Thyatira needs some of what Ephesus has, the testing of the teachers and prophets to find the true ones from the false ones.

Thyatira has a shark in the water, a snake in the grass. A prophetess whom John names "Jezebel." In the Old Testament, Jezebel was the wife of King Ahab who encouraged Israel to worship Baal and sent posses and lynch mobs after the prophet Elijah. This Jezebel at Thyatira is luring the church into immorality and sacrilegious activities.

27

Thyatira had a wool and dyeing industry. Lydia was from Thyatira. While emperor worship and Roman religion were not so strong in Thyatira, the guilds were. We would say, "It's union rules." Guild meetings and dinners would include a sacrifice to the Emperor or the Roman gods, and the meat sacrificed would be served to the guild members. The choice was to join the guilds or not have a job. The economic pressure would have been tremendous.

While John's Revelation gives warning and encouragement against persecution and dangers to the church from outside, he is most alarmed at threats from the inside. People with the best of intentions can be drawn down the wrong paths for so many of the right reasons.

They need some kind of sunscreen to block out harmful rays. They need to be careful whose advice they buy and wary of those who give it.

For John of Patmos, the victory of the Lord at the end of time is sure and certain, and there is comfort for the believers, and an uncounted multitude will be saved. He warns Ephesus that for some, the lampstand will be removed. For Smyrna he has the promise of a crown of life for the faithful. For Pergamum he promises the hidden manna and the new name on the white stone. To Thyatira he offers the bright morning star, which is Jesus, the Lamb, whose sacrifice ushers in a new day.

For this Lent, we have a vision of the Lord of the Church who knows our suffering because he has given his blood for us, and it is in his name that we have patient endurance, test all who come among us, and constantly renew our enthusiasm in faith, even to being different from the world around us. And with Thyatira, we can't stand by and tolerate corrupting influences. When we find a fraud or a scam, we need to denounce it. Thyatira had its Jezebel; who is leading us astray? It could be someone making you afraid to let your light shine.

Marianne Williamson said in her 1992 book, *A Return to Love*:

> *Our deepest fear is not that we are inadequate. Our deepest fear is that we are powerful beyond measure. It is our light, not our darkness, that most frightens us.*

We ask ourselves, who am I to be brilliant, gorgeous, talented and fabulous? Actually, who are you not to be? You are a child of God. Your playing small doesn't serve the world. There is nothing enlightened about shrinking so that other people won't feel insecure around you. We are born to make manifest the glory of God that is within us. It's not just in some of us; it's in everyone. And as we let our own light shine, we unconsciously give other people permission to do the same. As we are liberated from our own fear, our presence automatically liberates others.

Now that's a sunscreen we can use, and advice we don't need to be wary of.

Lord, help us to resist corruption and say no to everything that makes it more difficult to say yes to you.

The Letter To Sardis

Pat and Mike were somberly looking over the casket that held their late good friend Liam.

"He's looking so good, dressed in that fine suit. He'll be the envy of all the fine folks in heaven," Pat said.

Mike said, "Faith and begorrah, don't ya know, he won't be going to heaven. He was an atheist."

Pat said, "'Tis a pity, that. Well, he'll be the envy of all the folks in the other place."

Mike said, "Faith and begorrah, you're forgetting what a fine man our friend Liam was. He was too good a man to be going to the other place."

Pat said, "Ah and you're right as rain, by all the saints." And they were quiet for another minute. Finally, Pat could stand the silence no longer and said, "'Tis a real pity then. All dressed up and havin' no place to go."

Actually, Liam and the church at Sardis have one thing in common. They look really good, maybe even the envy of the churches, but they are both dead inside.

About 550 years before Christ, when Israel was in captivity to Babylon, Cyrus of Persia was conquering the Medes on his way to conquering the world. The book of Isaiah calls Cyrus the messiah, the anointed of God. He was a benevolent conqueror, and eventually conquered Babylon and sent the Babylonian Captives of Israel home.

On his way to do that, Cyrus conquered a kingdom called Lydia, and captured the king of Lydia, Croesus. Croesus was legendary for his wealth and riches. He lived in the capital of Lydia, Sardis. Legend says that the political philosopher of Athens, Solon, visited Croesus at Sardis. Croesus, in a manner of bragging about his power and riches, asked Solon if he thought such a rich man would be the happiest of men. Solon said, "Call no man happy before his death."

About eleven years into his reign, Cyrus captured Croesus. One of the many legends about Croesus says that Cyrus was making ready to burn him alive. That's when Croesus called out to Solon about his wise words. Solon wasn't there, so Cyrus asked Croesus what he meant. Cyrus liked the wisdom of Solon and Croesus' memory of it, and ordered the fire doused. Cyrus' men couldn't put out the fire, but the god Apollo sent a storm that put it out.

At any rate, we know from history that Croesus became a puppet king under Cyrus, and was the last king of Lydia.

Six hundred and fifty years later, Sardis has been conquered and destroyed a couple more times, and restored by the generosity of another emperor, this time the Roman, Tiberius Caesar. And there is a church there, and it is to this church that the fifth letter of Revelation is written.

The Romans have put John on their prison island, Patmos. The Spirit calls John to write to the seven churches in Asia Minor which lie on a circular road, like the round trip a missionary would make to end up near his home. He couches his report in colorful language, cradled in his vision of the risen Lord who is the Lamb who was slain for the sins of the world.

He has a vision of a glorious Jesus in a white robe amidst seven golden lampstands and holding seven stars. Jesus explains that the stars are the angels of the seven churches and the lampstands are the seven churches.

In the Sermon on the Mount, Jesus calls us to be the light of the world, a city set on a hill, a lampstand that is not hidden under a bushel. Here in Revelation, the Lord Christ stands among the lampstands and he holds the angels of the churches in his hand.

- Ephesus, the loveless church
- Smyrna, the persecuted church
- Pergamum, the compromising church
- Thyatira, the corrupt church
- Sardis, the dead church

- Philadelphia, the faithful church
- Laodicea, the lukewarm church

In the first letter, the Lord calls the church at Ephesus to task for being the fruit of shallow soil; they began with much love and great and good works, but they have lost their zeal. About the only thing in their favor is that they are pure. They test everyone and find out the false apostles and teachers.

The letter to the Smyrna church is short and glowing in praise for the small church that bravely faces death.

The church at Pergamum he criticizes for accepting the immorality and practices of the culture around them, adultery, and idol worship. He tells them to avoid even the appearance of evil, because others may not be so discerning in their vision. The strong need to set examples for the weak.

The church at Thyatira has grown in their good works. Love and faith and service and endurance have exceeded what they had at first. But they have a Jezebel that corrupts them.

The church at Sardis looks really good. They have the confidence of Croesus bragging to Solon. "Faith and begorrah," they are the envy of all the churches. But the Lord who has the seven stars, the angels of the churches says, "I know your works, you have the name of being alive, and you are dead."

They have some wonderful things in their church: apathy, indifference, and self-satisfaction. Things you can't identify easily, but which you can use to deceive yourself. They look alive, but they are dead inside. Like a mighty oak that looks strong but has a bug or disease inside that is killing it.

In this letter, John's words come very close to sounding like the Gospels. Awake, arise, revive, remember, repent! Jesus will come like a thief, and you will not know at what hour he will come upon you. Matthew, Mark, and Luke all quote Jesus with words like this.

In the Sermon on the Mount, Jesus says, "Not every one who says to me, 'Lord, Lord,' shall enter the kingdom of heaven, but he who does the will of my Father who is in heaven" (Matthew 7:21).

Words are not enough. What you believe is not as important as the difference it makes that you believe.

A church tends to have a personality. It gets into habits, maybe even ruts. Lyle Schaller, a consultant on church administration, says a church does what it has the most practice doing. Ephesus has endurance. Smyrna has faith and courage in the face of persecution. Pergamum has compromised itself with the society around it. Thyatira follows its Jezebel down the garden path. Sardis has mastered the art of looking alive when really it is dead.

So the message here is to analyze our habit. We must ask ourselves: What is it we do with routine acceptance that may not be in the Spirit of the Lamb who gives his life in sacrifice for the church and those who walk with him in white? For no church is all bad. Even Sardis has some names still written in the Lamb's book of life, "People who have not soiled their garments ... for they are worthy." Now what is it that makes them worthy? They may not be worthy in themselves, but the Lamb who is worthy has made them worthy. For Revelation, that makes the Lamb worthy. And he who conquers surrenders to the leading of God's Spirit, makes the good confession with courage and without lapsing, and sacrifices his life in love.

Helen Keller lived from 1880 to 1968. From the age of two she was deaf and blind, and the story of her rehabilitation is legendary. Deaf and blind all her life, she was still one of the most alive and vital persons in history. One of the great things she said was this:

> *I believe that we can live on earth according to the teachings of Jesus, and that the greatest happiness will come to the world when [each person] obeys His commandment, "Love one another."*
>
> *I believe that every question between [people] is a religious question, and that every social wrong is a moral wrong....*
>
> *I believe that life is given us so that we may grow in love, and I believe that God is in me as the sun is in the color and fragrance of a flower — the light in my darkness, the Voice in my silence.*

Now there's a person who has a habit of being alive! Make that your creed, your motto for living, and no one will have to say, "'Tis a real pity then. All dressed up and havin' no place to go."

For John of Patmos, the victory of the Lord at the end of time is sure and certain, and there is comfort for the believers, and an uncounted multitude will be saved. He warns Ephesus that for some, the lampstand will be removed. They could lose their church. They could lose their salvation. For Smyrna he has the promise of a crown of life for the faithful. For Pergamum he promises the hidden manna and the new name on the white stone. To Thyatira he offers the bright morning star, which is Jesus, the Lamb, whose sacrifice ushers in a new day. To Sardis he promises the white garment of purity, and to confess his name before the Father and before his angels.

For this Lent, we have a vision of the Lord of the Church who knows our suffering because he has given his blood for us, and it is in his name that we have patient endurance, test all who come among us, constantly renew our enthusiasm in faith, certain we are different from the world around us, awake and alive in Christ. All dressed up, and knowing where we're going.

Lord, make us alive, keeping us from deceiving ourselves, and help us to say no to everything that makes it more difficult to say yes to you.

The Letter To Philadelphia

Where was the Declaration of Independence signed? Everyone knows this. At the bottom! Of course!

Well, the students of history among us will say it was signed at Philadelphia. It's a great city in Pennsylvania, the fifth largest in the United States, once capital of our country. The Constitution was also written and signed there. It has been called the birthplace of the nation. It's also called "The City of Brotherly Love." That's what the name means in Greek: "Brotherly love."

But there used to be two other Philadelphias. One was in Lydia, now Turkey, in Asia Minor. At the time John writes the book of Revelation, this Philadelphia is only about 200 years old, the youngest city of John's seven churches. It was built by Attalus II, a king of Pergamum. Attalus' love of his brother Eumenes earned him the name "he who loves his brother." And this is the name of the city he founded.

It was part of God's plan that the Lord of love came into the first century, a time not known for its brotherly love.

The Romans have put John on their prison island, Patmos. The Spirit calls John to write to the seven churches in Asia Minor he must have visited as a missionary because he knows them so well. He couches his message in artistic language, cradled in his vision of the risen Lord who transcends anything we know.

He has a vision of a magnificent Jesus in a white robe amidst seven golden lampstands and holding seven stars. Jesus explains that the stars are the angels of the seven churches and the lampstands are the seven churches.

In the Sermon on the Mount, Jesus calls us to be the light of the world, a city set on a hill, a lampstand that is not hidden under a bushel. Here in Revelation, the Lord Christ stands among the lampstands and he holds the angels of the churches in his hand.

- Ephesus, the loveless church
- Smyrna, the persecuted church
- Pergamum, the compromising church
- Thyatira, the corrupt church
- Sardis, the dead church
- Philadelphia, the faithful church
- Laodicea, the lukewarm church

In the first letter, the Lord calls the church at Ephesus to task for being the fruit of shallow soil; they began with much love and great and good works, but they have lost their zeal. About the only thing in their favor is that they are pure. They test everyone and find out the false apostles and teachers.

The second letter to the Smyrna church is short and glowing in praise for the small church that bravely faces death.

The church at Pergamum he criticizes for accepting the immorality and practices of the culture around them, adultery, and idol worship. He tells them to avoid even the appearance of evil, because others may not be so discerning in their vision. The strong need to set examples for the weak.

The church at Thyatira has grown in their good works. Love and faith and service and endurance have exceeded what they had at first. But they have a Jezebel that corrupts them.

The church at Sardis looks really good. They look alive, but they are dead inside.

There is no word of criticism for the church at Philadelphia. They are the most faithful of the seven. And they did it with no great size and no great power.

The only negative the Lord tells John to write in their letter is that they have among them people of the lie, people of the synagogue of Satan who lie. As in the other letters, there is always the possibility that some in the church are hypocrites. They look and act like believers, but something is wrong inside. They try to lead the church astray, like the false prophets and teachers the church at Ephesus is famous for testing, or the Jezebel at Thyatira. The letter to Smyrna mentions the same problem in the same words.

If even the faithful church at Philadelphia is warned of people who hide their evil, we don't have to be ashamed when we lack brotherly love here. But his point is: Who is the real chosen of God? Those of any stripe or race or color who by their lives show the love of God — who have God's name written on them — these are the truly faithful.

There is an incident in the life of Jesus that most Christians tend to ignore or gloss over. Jesus is teaching at Capernaum just after he called the disciples. Controversies arise and some think he has a demon, and some think he comes from the devil. Pretty soon his mother and his brothers and sisters arrive at his home. They think he is "beside himself" or we might say, "Out of this mind." It may just be that they are concerned for his health. At any rate, the crowds are so great the family can't get in, so they send word. When Jesus hears that his mother and brothers and sisters want to talk to him, he points to his disciples and says, "Here are my mother and my brothers! For whoever does the will of my Father in heaven is my brother, and sister, and mother" (Matthew 12:49; Mark 3:35).

In the Sermon on the Mount, Jesus says, "Not every one who says to me, 'Lord, Lord,' shall enter the kingdom of heaven, but he who does the will of my Father who is in heaven" (Matthew 7:21).

Words are not enough. What you believe is not as important as the difference it makes in your life that you believe.

A church tends to have a personality. It gets into habits, maybe even ruts. Lyle Schaller, a consultant on church administration, says a church does what it has the most practice doing. Ephesus has endurance. Smyrna has faith and courage in the face of persecution. Pergamum has compromised itself with the society around it. Thyatira follows its Jezebel down the garden path. Sardis has mastered the art of looking alive when really it is dead. Philadelphia is faithful, and makes the most of its size and lack of power.

So the message here is to analyze our habit. Ask ourselves: What is it we do with routine acceptance that may not be in the spirit of brotherly love and the fatherhood of God?

The church at Philadelphia is the church of the open doors. Note verses 7 and 8: "The words of the holy one, the true one, who has the key of David, who opens and no one shall shut, who shuts and no one shall open. I know your works. Behold, I have set before you an open door, which no one is able to shut."

An open door is an opportunity, a mission, a chance to serve, a purpose, a goal. I think this is the habit of the church of Philadelphia; they have the knack of finding a vacuum to fill, of seeing the needs of people around them and meeting them, of making their obstacles into opportunities. They don't worry about their weakness because they know the power of God in whom they believe and in whose name and by whose power they act. They live in faith. That's a good habit to have.

For John of Patmos, the victory of the Lord at the end of time is sure and certain, and there is comfort for the believers, and an uncounted multitude will be saved. He warns Ephesus that for some, the lampstand will be removed. They could lose their church. They could lose their salvation. For Smyrna he has the promise of a crown of life for the faithful. For Pergamum he promises the hidden manna and the new name on the white stone. To Thyatira he offers the bright morning star, which is Jesus, the Lamb, whose sacrifice ushers in a new day. To Sardis he promises the white garment of purity, and to confess his name before the Father and before his angels. For the believers at Philadelphia he will write on them three things: the name of God, the name of the city of God, and Jesus' own new name. He will make them pillars of the temple of God, and never shall they go out of it.

We have a vision of the Lord of the Church who knows our suffering because he has given his blood for us, and it is in his name that we have patient endurance, test all who come among us, constantly renew our enthusiasm in faith, certain we are different from the world around us, awake and alive in Christ to the door that is open and that no one can shut.

Now, at Philadelphia, Pennsylvania, in 1776, the signers of the Declaration of Independence pledged their lives, their fortunes, and their sacred honor. They saw a need, a vacuum to fill, and put their lives on the line to meet that need, to fill that vacuum. What open doors are there around us this Lent? The Lord is calling us as pillars of his temple to make a difference in our part of his world.

Lord, open our doors and never let them shut to those who say no to everything that makes it more difficult to say yes to you.

The Letter To Laodicea

I was reading a murder mystery the other day, a really complex novel, layered with meaning. And I noticed that the story didn't really turn on whodunit or why they dunnit, but on the relationships of the characters. And what tipped me off was a line that was repeated a few times. How many people do you really get close to in your life? And the answer is maybe three or four, and the really important ones are the relationships you form early in life, in the formative years, high school, junior high, college, early career. The implication being when you get older than that, it's too late. You get the idea that you don't need anybody.

My buddy in high school was named Paul. As I look back, our relationship revolved around the music of the early '60s. He was always coming up with some new song or record, and I hadn't heard it. He would quote lines from it, and I would be mystified that he drew meaning from some simple lyrics.

One of these I remember plainly is a Simon and Garfunkel song. Paul quoted lines to me: "I have no need for friendship; friendship causes pain. I am a rock, I am an island." The point of the song was the best you could do was hurt no one, and let no one hurt you. What you don't immediately see is the pattern of Simon and Garfunkel. Sometimes they made the ugly attractive so you would look at it. And then they made it plain. It's ugly.

Nothing is so ugly as the person who thinks he doesn't need anyone else. He's self-sufficient. He doesn't risk loving because loving means to need someone, and he doesn't. "A rock feels no pain. And an island never cries."

In 61 A.D. the city of Laodicea was destroyed by an earthquake. Not unusual in that part of the world. Sardis and Philadelphia were both hit by earthquakes in 17 A.D. Both of these cities got government aid to rebuild. Sardis got tax relief and Philadelphia got subsidies. But in 61 Laodicea refused the Emperor's help and rebuilt their city on their own. Proud folks. We don't need anybody. I am a rock; I am an island.

And the Lord says, "That's what's wrong with you." Look at verse 17. "You say I am rich, I have prospered, and I need nothing; not knowing that you are wretched, pitiable, poor, blind, and naked." They *have* so much, they don't know what they *need*.

John seems to know a lot about Laodicea. It was a wealthy manufacturing center. It was famous for raven black wool, and wool clothes, and a salve for healing the eyes. Laodicea had a natural water supply, too. It came from a hot spring and was channeled over a distance. When it reached Laodicea it was no longer hot, but it hadn't had time to get cold. It was tepid.

Poetically the Lord advises Laodicea to come to him for *white* garments, eye salve, and a different kind of riches. Garments to cover their shame, salve that they may truly see, and riches refined by fire.

They have become like their water, neither hot nor cold. They are proud, self-satisfied, and apathetic. Being neither hot nor cold doesn't cultivate relationships. Standing in the middle of the road means you get run over from both ways. With the Lord, there is no tepid; there is only hot or cold.

The Lord says to Laodicea, "I will spew you out of my mouth." Actually the word here is even more harsh than spew. Basically he's saying, "You make me sick."

Look at how harsh he is to Laodicea! Not only "spew out," but I stand outside your church. "I stand at the door and knock." It's a shame they don't know they will be expelled and they don't know Christ the Lord is outside their fellowship and not among them. They think they are fine folks.

You know that famous painting of Jesus standing at the door knocking? Have you ever looked at it closely? There is a message there in the painting. Jesus is standing on the outside and knocking to get in. But there is no handle on the outside of the door. *You* have to open the door. You want a relationship that is warm, you seek that person's company, you do warm things toward him. Same with the Lord.

But the good news here is that "if any one hears my voice and opens the door, I will come in to him and eat with him, and he with me. He who conquers, I will grant him to sit with me on my throne, as I myself conquered and sat down with my Father on his throne." As always in Revelation we have to look behind the words and see what they actually mean. "He who conquers" has been the key word that has popped up in all the letters. How does a Christian conquer? How does Christ conquer?

It is not evident on first reading this fantastic book that the conquering is just what we are here to celebrate in Holy Week. The life, death, and resurrection of Jesus in giving his holy and precious blood that we might live.

Revelation can be seen as a play in seven acts, each act with seven scenes. The vision of the seven letters is one act, each letter is one scene. In the next act John is in the throne room of heaven, and the Lord God has a scroll sealed with seven seals. He wants to know who is worthy to open the scroll and break the seals. John weeps because in all of heaven's throne room no one is worthy. An angel announces the Lion of Judah. Instead, John sees a Lamb. And all who are in the throne room sing, "You are worthy to take the scroll and to open its seals, for you were slaughtered and by your blood you ransomed for God saints from every tribe and language and people and nation; you have made them to be a kingdom and priests serving our God and they will reign on earth" (5:9-10).

The Lord of the Church, who stands among the lampstands and holds the stars of the churches in his hand, is the Lamb!

In the first letter, the Lord calls the church at Ephesus to task for being the fruit of shallow soil; they began with much love and great and good works, but they have lost their zeal.

The second letter to the Smyrna church is short and glowing in praise for the small church that bravely faces death.

The church at Pergamum he criticizes for accepting the culture around them, adultery, and idol worship. He tells them to avoid even the appearance of evil, because others may not be so discerning in their vision. The strong need to set examples for the weak.

45

The church at Thyatira has grown in their good works. But they have a Jezebel that corrupts them.

The church at Sardis looks really good. They look alive, but they are dead inside.

The small, weak church at Philadelphia is the most faithful of the seven. And they did it with no great size and no great power.

Laodicea is the lukewarm church, and for this it gets the harshest treatment, because the church is life and death, and you must be either hot or cold; there is no in between.

For John of Patmos, the victory of the Lord at the end of time is sure and certain, and there is comfort for the believers, and an uncounted multitude will be saved. He warns Ephesus that for some, the lampstand will be removed. They could lose their church. They could lose their salvation. For Smyrna he has the promise of a crown of life for the faithful. For Pergamum he promises the hidden manna and the new name on the white stone. To Thyatira he offers the bright morning star, which is Jesus, the Lamb, whose sacrifice ushers in a new day. To Sardis he promises the white garment of purity, and to confess his name before the Father and before his angels. For the believers at Philadelphia he will write on them three things: the name of God, the name of the city of God, and Jesus' own new name. He will make them pillars of the temple of God, and never shall they go out of it. He invites Laodicea to open the door, and all who conquer will sit on the throne with Jesus and the Father.

We have a vision of the Lord of the Church who knows our suffering because he has given his blood for us, and it is in his name that we have patient endurance, test all who come among us, constantly renew our enthusiasm in faith, certain we are different from the world around us, awake and alive in Christ to the door that is open and that no one can shut.

How many close relationships can you have in a lifetime? You can have a lifetime close relationship with Jesus, the Lamb who was slain, because it is he who conquers, in spite of the betraying, the denying, the abandoning, and the crucifying. In fact, because of it. Open yourself to him. Spend time with him, your friend Jesus.

In prayer. In meditation. In study of scripture. Follow in his steps. Giving yourself, your life, a gift to the world.

Lord, keep us warm and close in our relationship to you, that we may say no to everything that makes it more difficult to say yes to you.

Revelation 5:1-13
Good Friday

What Is Revealed?

In that wonderful old movie, High Noon, *Gary Coo-
per is Will Kane, marshal of a small, rough town on
the prairie. He has cleaned up the town, and not everybody likes it cleaned up. Well, he's getting married.
His bride is a Quaker, and she's persuaded him to hang
up his guns and his star and move to a town a hundred
miles away to run a store.*

*Just then, the townspeople hear that Frank Miller
has been pardoned for his murder conviction and will
be arriving in town on the noon train. The new marshal won't be in town until tomorrow and none of his
old deputies can handle this. And no one in town will
help. No one will stand up to the outlaw and his friends,
even when they think Will Kane can do it by himself,
and only needs the backing, they still won't do it. Some
won't just because they liked it the way it was. Some
think if they stay out of it they won't be bothered.*

*In one scene Kane walks out of the door of the jail
into the center of the dusty street and there is only silence. Even the girl who was supposed to love him
turned her back.*

*Everyone wants him to quit, to turn back, to run
away. Kane only wants to do the right thing because it
is the right thing. But he has to do it alone.*

*Why is it that the righteous person is so often alone?
In the words of an old gospel song, "You got to walk that
lonesome valley; You got to walk it for yourself. Nobody
else can walk it for you; You got to walk it for yourself."*
(Mosley, *Emphasis*, March-April, 2000, p. 71)

The answer in the book of Revelation is that you are not alone.
Except for John himself, who really does nothing but narrate, and
Jesus and the angels, there is no individual who stands out as a
personality in Revelation. John wants us to see the sweep of God's

plan for salvation as it affects the whole of humankind. He writes to churches, not individuals, and while the individuals may be facing persecution, they do not face it alone. The good news of Revelation is: We are not alone, even when we feel alone.

That may be why Revelation is so hard for some to understand. They feel alone, and any argument or statement that you are not alone has to be wrong.

And here is a paradox for us. The real hero of Revelation is Jesus Christ, and he is pictured in glory, coming in power to bring salvation and life for the believers, and judgment and defeat for the unrighteous, unbelieving, and evil. And he is that because he died alone.

In his vision, John sees a holy scroll, the book of the last judgment. It is sealed with seven seals and no one is found worthy to open the seals. He weeps because people, even the people of God, are sinful and unworthy of holy things. But then he sees the One who is worthy. And why is he worthy? Because he is the Lamb who was slain, who died as a sacrifice for the sins of the world. Everywhere John sees people who have their robes washed in the blood, and his blood is what makes them worthy. And there are hosts of angels around Jesus, "And they sang a new song: 'You are worthy to take the scroll and to open its seals, because you were slain, and with your blood you bought for God people from every tribe and language and people and nation. You have made them to be a kingdom and priests to serve our God, and they will reign on the earth.' "

What is revealed in Revelation is precisely what is revealed on Golgotha on Good Friday. The one who dies alone dies there that we might know that wherever we are, we are not alone.

Why did Jesus have to die?

Well, there have been many answers to this question. One is that Jesus challenged the people in power and they obliterated him as they would any obstacle in their path. Jerusalem "killing the prophets." Another is that the ruler of this world must kill any good that it cannot corrupt. You probably know people who can't stand to see anyone "better" than they are, and they put them down to make themselves look better.

But the all-time answer is sin. The wages of sin is death. A death is required to answer for the sin of the world. The catch is that it can't be just any death. The life given must be worthy. And that's what John is weeping over. No one of us is worthy. But there is one who is worthy, and that one is willing to give his life.

And that really is the gospel message. The message is that life is for the giving away. We exist, not for self-preservation, or survival, or to prevail, or to win contests, or to amass a fortune, but to give ourselves away. He is greatest among us who will give himself away most completely. No mere human being could do that. It would take a god. And not a god like the Greeks and Romans had, but one who was willing to leave his heaven and godhood behind, and give it, and himself, away.

Jesus does that.

The Lamb who was slain has begun his reign, but this is *how* it begins, on a cross, with blood and death. And you know, we do have to come to this kingdom alone, as individuals walking our lonesome valleys by ourselves. But when we do, we find ourselves at the foot of the cross with the uncounted multitude that John sees, the saints who have gone before, and all the angels, because the Lamb was slain, that we might know we are not alone.

In Colossians 1:24, Paul writes, "I am now rejoicing in my sufferings for your sake, and in my flesh I am completing what is lacking in Christ's afflictions for the sake of his body, that is the church." I've always wondered about that. What is lacking in Christ's sacrifice? Well, we have an answer here in the new song of the four living creatures and the 24 elders with the harps and the golden bowls falling down before the lamb. They sing, "You have made them to be a kingdom and priests to serve our God, and they will reign on the earth."

If no less a minister and missionary than Paul says he is completing what is lacking in Christ's sacrifice, then something is lacking. But both Paul and Revelation agree that we are saved by the sacrifice of the Lamb. So what is lacking is our response to the sacrifice. Peter calls all believers "a kingdom of priests, a holy nation, God's own people, that you may proclaim the mighty acts of him who called you out of darkness into his marvelous light" (1 Peter 2:9).

51

Paul points to his own imprisonment and sufferings because they demonstrate to the Colossians, and the Laodiceans, and the Thessalonians, and the Corinthians, and the Romans, and all those other folks, that this man who suffered and died on a cross did that for the people — and if Paul did not say so, and himself participate in the suffering of Christ, those people would not know that they are saved by grace through faith in Christ Jesus. Nor would we.

And there's something lacking in Christ's sacrifice as long as there are people around us who don't know about his sacrifice. We supply what is lacking, by giving a witness — and in that way we participate in his life, death, and resurrection.

When you worship in this church, or any Christian church, you give a witness. When you support a congregation with time, talent, or money, you give a witness. When you help someone in need, you give a witness. When you tell someone about your faith in Christ Jesus, you give a witness. When you meet a challenge in your life, such as suffering, sickness, or loss, you give a witness. When you champion a righteous cause when it would be so easy to ignore it, you give a witness. When you return meanness and cruelty with kindness and courtesy, you give a witness. When you are the best you can be in spite of the temptations to be less, you give a witness. If you can quote more Bible verses from memory than television commercials, you give a witness.

And that is joining in the songs of the angels and the countless multitudes of heaven, the great cloud of witnesses, that John of Patmos sees in his vision of heaven, singing, "To him who sits on the throne and to the Lamb be praise and honor and glory and power, for ever and ever." That is praise of the Lamb, and that is what is lacking, and we can supply it, because we are not alone.

It may be "high noon," and the streets are deserted, but we know the Christ and him crucified, and we know all the witnesses to his cross through the ages.

Lord, help us to know that we are not alone, no matter what, for you died that we might say no to everything that would keep us from saying yes to you.

The Hallelujah Chorus

In 1741, a 56-year-old German living in England was at the lowest point in his career. He was awkward, overweight, had abnormally big hands and feet, and didn't speak very well, mixing the King's English with German, Italian, and French. He had suffered a stroke and was partially paralyzed on his left side. At the time, the popular entertainment was opera and oratorios, and this man wrote some very popular ones. He even wrote some biblical ones, one about Esther, and another about Saul, and one about Israel in Egypt. Old Testament stuff. But the audiences of the time could be cruel. They didn't stop with loud talking; they would play cards, ostentatiously walk around, and eat snacks impolitely.

Operas and oratorios were the movies and television shows of that time, and it took money to produce them, and they didn't always make money. This composer suffered some financial setbacks, scathing criticism, and a decline in popularity. So one night in 1741 he went out for a walk, an unusual act in itself. He was depressed and needed to think. In spite of the fact he had become a naturalized English citizen, he was trying to decide whether to give it up and move back to Germany.

He needed a rebirth.

This night time walk has become a legend. The legend says the partially paralyzed composer walked all night and returned home when it was nearly morning. At home he found a thick envelope from the man who wrote the librettos for his music — the book, or text, the words, to the operas and oratorios. This envelope had only scripture texts in it. Bible verses.

The exhausted composer read the texts, then went to bed. But he couldn't sleep. He was seized by new energy, new life. For three weeks he worked tirelessly on the music for this new oratorio, hardly eating.

When he had finished, he had in his hands probably the best known and most performed oratorio in music history. It didn't make him any money — he gave the proceeds to charity. But the work did give him new life, new hope, and faith that sustained him the rest of his life.

He was George Frederick Handel, and the oratorio was *The Messiah.*

I don't think it's a risk to say that Handel's *Messiah* has been performed every Easter since 1741, by someone somewhere.

If you can't get in the mood for Easter, just listen to Handel's *Messiah.* It says Easter all through it. In fact, if you want to understand Revelation, read it while listening to *The Messiah.* Especially the Hallelujah Chorus.

John's Revelation of the New Heaven and the New Earth is chock full of singing. In almost every scene there is some heavenly chorus singing something. You could take out all the choruses in Revelation and put them together without the narrative, and have the theme of the book. God is the one to be praised, and him alone, and the Lamb is also worthy to be praised because of the giving of his blood in righteousness for all believers.

Listen to some of the choruses from Revelation, especially in chapters 5, 15, and 19:

> *You are worthy to take the scroll and to open its seals, because you were slain, and with your blood you purchased men for God from every tribe and language and people and nation. You have made them to be a kingdom and priests to serve our God, and they will reign on the earth.* (5:9-10)

"The kingdom of the world has become the kingdom of our Lord and of his Christ, and he will reign for ever and ever." (5:15)

> *Great and marvelous are your deeds, Lord God Almighty. Just and true are your ways, King of the ages. Who will not fear you, O Lord, and bring glory to your name? For you alone are holy. All nations will come*

and worship before you, for your righteous acts have been revealed. (15:3b-4)

Some of the choruses in Revelation are dark and mournful, filled with woe and sorrow, but mostly they sound like this. And here's one more:

> *Hallelujah! For our Lord God Almighty reigns. Let us rejoice and be glad and give him glory! For the wedding of the Lamb has come, and his bride has made herself ready. Fine linen, bright and clean, was given her to wear.* (Fine linen stands for the righteous acts of the saints.) (19:6c-8)

John of Patmos gives us the original Hallelujah Chorus. "Hallelujah" means "praise God," using a derivative of the name of God given in the Old Testament. This word is used in the Bible only in the Psalms and here in this chapter of Revelation. And in most modern translations, it only appears as "Hallelujah" here in Revelation. In the modern versions of the Psalms, it is usually rendered "Praise the Lord."

In the last book of the Bible, John the elder has a great vision of the earth ending in subjection to God's will. He sees a great tribulation full of cataclysmic events, persecution, and suffering. But after all the destruction, even in the midst of the suffering, out of the ashes of the fires and the blood and sweat and tears of the persecutions, comes a new heaven and a new earth, and God the Lord takes the church as his bride in new life.

The worship and praise of Christ is central. This praise arises out of the joy of salvation, rather than the fear of doom. And that is precisely the hymn of the multitude in heaven: Salvation belongs to our God who sits upon the throne, and to the Lamb!

Revelation gives us a picture of great purity. Everything is white and shining, or golden and jeweled, like jasper. There is even a woman clothed with the sun. But it also delights in strikingly contradictory pictures, like television commercials that show luxury sedans sitting alone on a bare mountaintop, with no road.

Or people talking underwater and not getting wet. It's an attention-getting device. You don't pay much attention to ordinary, commonplace images you see everyday. You get jaded.

Here in chapter 19, we have one of those contrasting pictures. The bride is clothed in righteousness and purity, and the wedding feast is ready. But the other woman with her, temptation and sin, is condemned and burned.

John is writing to a church under persecution, and in his vision the persecutors, Babylon and Rome, sin and death and the power of the devil, will be defeated and destroyed. And there is joy and rejoicing in heaven and on earth.

You've probably heard or seen the "Footprints" story about the man who dreamed of his life with Jesus, and when he felt most alone Jesus said, "That's when I carried you." There is much truth and comfort in that story. But it's not the whole story.

You and Jesus are walking down the road together. For much of the way, the Lord's footprints go along steadily, consistently, rarely varying the pace. But your prints are a disorganized stream of zigzags, starts, stops, turnarounds, circles, departures, and returns.

Gradually, your footprints come more in line with the Lord's, soon paralleling his consistently. You and Jesus walk as true friends.

This seems perfect, but then your footprints that were next to the Master's are now walking precisely in his steps. Inside his larger footprints is the small "sandprint," safely enclosed. You and Jesus are becoming one.

This goes on for many miles. But gradually you notice another change. The footprint inside the larger footprint grows larger. Eventually it disappears altogether. There is only one set of footprints. They become one.

Again, this goes on for a time. But then something awful happens. The second set of footprints is back. And this time it seems even worse. Zigzags everywhere. Stops. Starts. Deep gashes in the sand. A mess of prints.

You ask, "Lord, I understand that when I was a new Christian, you walked on through the storm and helped me learn to walk with you. And when the smaller footprints were inside yours, I was learning to walk in your steps. I followed you very closely.

Then I suppose that I was actually growing so much that I was becoming like you in every way. But did I regress or something? The footprints went back to two, and this time it was worse than the first."

The Lord smiles, then laughs. "You didn't know?" he says. "That was when we danced."

This Easter sing, "Allelujah!" Walk with a spring in your step and a smile on your face! Celebrate life! Rejoice in your baptism! For the Lord our God omnipotent reigneth! King of kings and Lord of lords! And he shall reign forever and ever! Allelujah!

Lord, we sing your praises, saying no to everything that makes it more difficult to say yes to you.

Vision From Patmos

*A cowboy was crossing the desert when his horse bit
the dust. He made it to a small desert town after a
day's walk. There was no stable, so he wearily put his
saddle on the boardwalk in front of the town's only
hitching post. A lone rider approached the hitching
post, dismounted from a large, gleaming white horse,
and tied the reins to the post. "Mister," the tired pe-
destrian said, "if you'll change that horse's brand, I'll
give you enough of these twenty dollar gold pieces for
a trip to Dodge." The rider said, "Stranger, if I could
change this horse's brand I'd already be in Dodge."*
(Mosley, *Emphasis*, March-April, 1998, p. 60)

I admire the fellow who says he has two rules he lives by. The
first one is, "Don't tell all you know." And he won't tell me the
second rule.

It seems that there is always something hidden. Some obstacle
in the paths we ride, such as a horse dying in the desert, or a horse
with the wrong brand, or having to be somewhere we don't want
to be, or with people we don't want to be with, or wanting to know
something but the person who knows can't or won't tell.

Almost all of these apply to John the elder. The Romans have
put John on their prison island, Patmos. The Spirit calls John to
write to the seven churches in Asia Minor which lie on a circular
road, like the round trip an evangelist or missionary would make
to end up near his home. He couches his message in symbolic
language, cradled in his vision of the risen Lord who transcends
anything in human experience.

The main point of his letter is in the three titles for Jesus he
gives in verse 5: The vision of Patmos is of Jesus the faithful witness, the firstborn of the dead, and the ruler of rulers on the earth.

A witness is one who gives evidence of something he has seen or experienced. You can be a witness to an accident, a crime, or an historical event. But the witness has to do more than just see or experience something. He has to tell about it. Jesus is the faithful witness. He tells us about his experience of God. And who better to tell about God than God's son? In John's Gospel, the writer calls Jesus the Word of God, the telling or expressing of God. The vision of Patmos is of Jesus, the faithful witness.

Many of us are uncomfortable with witnessing about Jesus. We might think that we do not know enough and are not sufficiently trained in order to know what to say. As a result, many are quite content to leave witnessing to the professionals, and they seldom say anything about their faith.

And then there's Clay Allison.

Clay Allison fought for the South in the Civil War, was captured as a spy, and escaped, and may have had a run-in with Marshal Wyatt Earp. Once he hijacked the Lone Wolf Saloon in Pecos City for about two hours to have church.

He got fifty or sixty folks into the bar, some at gunpoint, made them sing a hymn, and then said it was time for prayer, everybody down!

He prayed: "O Lord! This yere's a mighty bad neck of woods. Make these fellers see that when they gits caught in the final round-up and drove over the last divide, they don't stan' no sort o' show to git to stay on the heavenly ranch 'nless they believes an' builds a house to pray and preach in. Right here I subscribes a hundred dollars to build a church, an' if airy one o' these fellers don' ante up accordin' to his means, O Lord, make it Your pers'n'l business to see that he wears the Devil's brand and earmark and never gits another drop o' good spring water.

"Of course, I allow You knows I don' sport no wings myself, but I want to do what's right ef You'll sort o' give me a shove the proper way. Clay Allison's got a fast horse an' is tol'able handy with his rope,

*and he's goin' to run these fellers into your corral even
if he has to rope an' drag 'em there. Amen. Everybody
git up!"* (Mosley, *Emphasis*, March-April, 1998, p. 50)

In all of today's scriptures, people are groping for ways to say
something about what they have encountered, what has happened
to change their lives. As they learn and as things become clear to
them, they are not hesitant to say it.

> *Revelation has the reputation of being a hard book to
> understand. Here's a specific example. There was a
> noted biblical scholar. A professor at a university. A
> pastor and a church leader. A man renowned in church
> history for his deep understanding of the Bible and the
> way he changed the church forever in the way we look
> at the message of scripture.*
>
> *Early in his life he wrote one page about the Rev-
> elation of John, saying it was so hard to understand
> that we might as well throw it out.*
>
> *Later he revised his thinking. This time the notes
> about Revelation took up ten pages. The times had
> changed. Now he reviewed the book in detail. Now he
> said, "... we can profit by this book and make good use
> of it. First, for our comfort! We can rest assured that
> neither force nor lies, neither wisdom nor holiness,
> neither tribulation nor suffering shall suppress Chris-
> tendom, but it will gain the victory and conquer at last."*
>
> *What made the difference? Hard times, opposi-
> tion, persecution. He had been branded an outlaw,
> burned in effigy by mobs, chased by posses, kidnapped
> by friends for his own safety, and exiled to live under
> an assumed name in disguise. But he put away his safe
> fortress of stone and his disguise to once again be-
> come the church leader he had been, and to find that
> the church of our Lord does stand victorious in the
> end in spite of all the world can throw against it.*
>
> *He was Martin Luther.* (Mosley, *Emphasis*, Janu-
> ary-February, 1998, p. 16)

Luther was saying what Jesus means to him. That's all that John of Patmos is saying. What Jesus means to him. He just has many different ways of saying it. But they all come from his culture. It's up to us to speak for our culture. Peter can deny, and Thomas can doubt, but each can also say in his own words what Jesus means to him. He can witness to Jesus.

The vision of Patmos is of Jesus the faithful witness, and the firstborn of the dead.

It's possible that John had some of the letters of Paul, maybe the one he sent to Corinth where he lists the witnesses to the resurrection. In baptism we participate in Christ's death. We participate also in his resurrection. We are made members of a new race with him. Jesus is the firstborn of the new race. Like most races, there is something about us that makes us different from the rest of humanity: we will rise to new life, as Jesus has done before us, the firstborn.

This is the joy of Easter, of waking to the idea that God loves us and there is nothing, not even death, that can stop that love.

The vision of Patmos is of Jesus the faithful witness, the firstborn of the dead, and the ruler of rulers on earth.

What rules us more than death? Any other threat to us is just a function of death or the fear of it — or maybe the fear that whatever we wanted to do won't get done before we die. But Jesus has conquered death. That was Easter.

What could Rome do to the early Christians? The only threat any ruler has is some form of imprisonment or death. It's how they assert their power in this earth. John says by his example, "Go ahead and do your worst. I serve a higher power." And he wrote his letter from prison and we have it to read today.

I think the thing that makes Revelation so hard to accept is its theology of the cross: It shows the world taking up the cross of the final tribulations (don't get away from me here, I don't take them literally), and while we might see the theology of the cross of Christ and its gift of salvation for us, we don't want to see the world suffering. Or throwing away its salvation because it won't be the kingdom of priests John sees in his vision.

The vision of Patmos is of Jesus the faithful witness, the first-born of the dead, and the ruler of rulers on earth. But it also says, "All tribes of the earth will wail on account of him." Even so, come, Lord Jesus.

The tribes of the earth crucified Jesus, put John in their prison, and tried to silence Luther. Jesus, John, and Luther gave a faithful witness. Can we do any less?

Lord, help us to give a faithful witness, saying no to everything that makes it more difficult to say yes to you.

Revelation 5:11-14
Easter 3

Living Creatures

Dakota tribal wisdom says that when you discover you are riding a dead horse, the best strategy is to dismount.

But in Texas we have other strategies for dead horses, including:

- Buying a stronger whip.
- Changing riders.
- Saying things like "This is the way we always have ridden this horse."
- Appointing a committee to study the horse.
- Arranging to visit other sites to see how they ride dead horses.
- Increasing the standards to ride dead horses.
- Appointing a tiger team to revive the dead horse.
- Creating a training session to increase our riding ability.
- Comparing the state of dead horses in today's environment.
- Enacting a policy declaring that "This horse is not dead."
- Blaming the horse's parents.
- Harnessing several dead horses together for increased speed.
- Declaring that "No horse is too dead to beat."
- Providing additional funding to increase the horse's performance.
- Do a study to see if contractors can ride it cheaper.
- Procure a COTS (Commercial Off The Shelf) dead horse.
- Declare the horse is "better, faster, and cheaper" dead.
- Form a quality circle to find uses for dead horses.
- Revisit the performance requirements for horses.
- Say "This horse was procured with cost as an independent variable."
- Close the horse farm where it was born.
- Promote the dead horse to a supervisory position.

- Commission a study to identify ways to improve the product through incremental enhancements, such as adding wheels.

I'm not talking about an old horse, which can still be useful, or deserves its rest. Part of the problem is that the dead horse did have a useful life, which we should give thanks for and rejoice over. But when its useful life is over, let it go. It is no longer a living creature, with the opportunity to learn and grow and the capacity to exult in its life and enjoy its work.

John the elder, in Revelation, pictures "four living creatures" before the throne. They puzzled me. John calls them, not just creatures, but *living* creatures, and then mentions *created things*, to contrast the things in creation that are living and the things that are inanimate objects.

Living creatures. The world is full of living creatures. The circle of life. Animals are one kind of living creatures. Human beings are another kind. What John is saying in his vision from Patmos is that every part of creation, living or not, praises God in heaven, or it isn't in heaven. And that's 24 hours a day.

John is saying that in heaven the worship of Christ is central, comes from every living creature, and is sevenfold praise.

The Romans have put John on their prison island, Patmos. The Spirit calls John to write to the seven churches in Asia Minor which lie on a circular road, like the round trip an evangelist or missionary would make to end up near his home. He couches his message in symbolic language, cradled in his vision of the risen Lord who transcends anything in human experience.

The main point of his letter is in the three titles for Jesus he gives in verse 5 of chapter 1: The vision of Patmos is of Jesus the faithful witness, the firstborn of the dead, and the ruler of rulers on the earth.

Scholars speculate that today's reading in chapter 5 reflects the liturgy of John's vision of heaven, which in turn influences the worship of the church of John's day. After God the Father appears and is praised, God the Son appears, and this paragraph is the praise he receives.

This story came from England: The Duchess called in one of the household employees. He stood stiffly at attention as she said in a stern voice, "Osborne, how long have you been with us? According to my records, you were employed to look after the dog."

Osborne said, "Yes, madam."

The Duchess went on, "Mrs. Bellamy tells me the dog died 27 years ago."

Osborne said, "Yes, madam. What would you like me to do now?"

Life has some purpose. We need to be asking continually, "What would you like me to do now?" Now what is more important than shaping ourselves for heaven?

There was a milk commercial that showed a guy newly arrived in what appears to be heaven. He has a chocolate chip cookie the size of Cookie Monster's head. He takes a bite, then notices a refrigerator. Hmmm, he says. He opens frig. It is (apparently) full of half-gallon cartons of milk. Yea! Then he opens one — it is empty. He quickly opens another ... empty again. And another and another and another ... Then he says, "Is this heaven, or is it...?"

We really can't know what either heaven or hell actually is; even the Bible can't tell us because they are vast unknowns. The human mind can't grasp either one. The most we can have is what we have here in Revelation: an approximation in word-pictures that give us some idea of heaven or hell.

And John's vision is that in heaven the worship of Christ is central and comes from every living creature.

Revelation can be broken down into a play with seven acts, each act having seven scenes. Act 1 deals with the church in this world, in John's time. In Act 2 we turn to the church in heaven. And there are some bizarre pictures here, but they are not all of John's making. The four living creatures described earlier in chapter 5 come from a vision of Ezekiel, and they have elements of the vision of angels in Isaiah's vision of the temple in heaven. So John carries us back to the Old Testament for some of his imagery.

What he's really saying is that God is the God of the living, in this world and the next. And what we do here, while living in this world, shapes us for the next.

Maybe the milk commercial can remind us that what we seek here on earth may wind up being an empty carton, if we don't fill our cartons with the nourishing, strengthening, filling praise of the living God.

One senior citizen said to the other, "I'm getting so old that my friends up in heaven must think I didn't make it." Don't think of it that way. Instead, consider it time to be used, to better shape yourself for the life to come, or to help shape this world into a better place to live.

C. S. Lewis, the English writer who devoted his life to Christian writing after converting from atheism, spoke of this in his book, *Mere Christianity*. He said that as we live and make our decisions we are being turned as a piece of wood is being turned on a lathe. But our turnings are not all one direction. We gather and lose speed. We change directions. Such is the human heart. In the end we wind up with the piece of work we take to all eternity, shaped by the turnings of life.

Frank Outlaw says it this way: "Watch your thoughts, they become words; watch your words, they become actions; watch your actions, they become habits; watch your habits, they become character; watch your character, for it becomes your destiny."

Our idea of the afterlife or heaven or hell will shape the way we shape ourselves for it. You may not be too thrilled with the picture John presents: just praise God in Christ for all eternity. But that's what he says. Could it be a picture that makes sense? It does if your life in this world tries to make every minute a practice for it: looking to Christ as central to life and his praise as its most important activity.

John is saying that in heaven the worship of Christ is central, comes from every living creature, and is sevenfold praise.

Look at the reading from Revelation in your bulletin. Find the praise given to the Lamb in verse 12, and count the praises he is given: "all power and wealth, wisdom and might, honor and glory and blessing!" Seven praises. Revelation uses the number 7 carefully and advisedly. It stands for completeness, wholeness. The Lamb was the animal given in sacrifice for sin, and John is here demonstrating that the sacrifice of Jesus was the whole and complete sacrifice. In him we have salvation. Nothing we do can add to that. It's whole and complete.

But what we can do to complete the sacrifice of Jesus is shape ourselves for a life of praise of God, here in this life and in the life to come. Today, and everyday, do seven things that praise God in Christ. Make your praise complete. That is shaping a life here that will be lived in heaven.

When what we do praises God, we don't have to worry about riding a dead horse. For we have the living Lamb who was slain, but now lives. If we are truly living creatures, we live to praise God in Christ, and will do so to all eternity. Praise God.

Lord, let us always give you all power and wealth, wisdom and might, honor and glory and blessing, saying no to everything that makes it more difficult to say yes to you.

Paradise Restored

In the last book of the Bible, John the elder has a great vision of the earth ending in subjection to God's will. He speaks of a great tribulation full of cataclysmic events, persecution, and suffering. It arrives gradually through the breaking of seven seals by the Lamb of God. But before the final seal is broken to usher in the terrible day of Lord's anger, the servants of God are sealed on their foreheads as a mark of their salvation, the ones who are allowed to stand before the Lord's wrath, numbering 144,000 of the tribes of Israel and more than can be counted from other nations. Theirs is the hope of paradise restored, and one of the elders in John's vision describes it.

What John is saying is:

1. We are lost from Paradise
2. which is restored by God through the Lamb.
3. The multitude praises God
4. and is comforted by the Lamb.

You find the main point of his letter in the three titles for Jesus he gives in verse 5 of his first chapter: the vision of Patmos is of Jesus the faithful witness, the firstborn of the dead, and the ruler of rulers on the earth. Further, he pictures a heaven where the worship of Christ is central, comes from every living creature, and is sevenfold praise.

This praise arises out of the joy of salvation, rather than the fear of doom. And that is precisely the hymn of the multitude in heaven: Salvation belongs to our God who sits upon the throne, and to the Lamb!

Martin Luther struggled with this idea. He wanted to know righteousness. He tried everything he could to put himself right with God. Then he came across a phrase of Paul's, in Romans, "the righteousness of God." And that phrase started the Reformation. We have no righteousness. It must come from God. And the

71

righteousness of God, his purpose, his aim, his glory, is to give us salvation. It is a gift of grace.

We are lost from Paradise which is restored by God through the Lamb. And the multitude praises God.

As we learned last Sunday, John shows us in his vision from Patmos that every part of creation, living or not, praises God in heaven. God is the God of the living, in this world and the next. And what we do here, while living in this world, shapes us for the next. Get the most out of this life and you'll get the most out of the next.

Look there at the reading for today. Find the praise given to God in verse 12, and count the praises he is given: "Blessing and glory and wisdom and thanksgiving and honor and power and might be to our God for ever and ever! Amen."

Almost the same as those given to the Lamb in chapter 5, last Sunday. "All power and wealth, wisdom and might, honor and glory and blessing!" Seven praises. Revelation uses the number 7 carefully and advisedly. It stands for completeness, wholeness. The Lamb was the animal given in sacrifice for sin, and John demonstrates in chapter 5 that the sacrifice of Jesus was the whole and complete sacrifice. In him we have salvation. Nothing we do can add to that. It's whole and complete. Here the praises given to God and the Lamb are given together. They are equally God.

But what of this multitude? John says that first he sees a crowd of 144,000; 12,000 for each of the twelve tribes of Israel. Some have claimed that this is the total number of spaces there are in heaven, and if you don't have one of the 144,000 tickets, you're out of luck. But John doesn't stop — God doesn't stop — with any number, or any country, or even the chosen nation of Israel. This multitude no one could count, from every nation, from all tribes and people and tongues, and he takes a breath and looks around to see if he missed anybody, all these folks in white robes that have been cleansed by the blood of the Lamb. Not cleansed by anything they have done. It's a gift of grace.

1. We are lost from Paradise
2. which is restored by God through the Lamb.
3. The multitude praises God
4. and is comforted by the Lamb.

The elder, or "interpreting angel," asks John, "Who are these?" And he answers his own question. These are they who have come out of the Great Tribulation; they have washed their robes and made them clean in the blood of the Lamb.

Revelation gives us a picture of great purity. Everything is white and shining, or golden and jeweled, like jasper. There is even a woman clothed with the sun. But it also delights in strikingly contradictory pictures, like television commercials that show luxury sedans sitting alone on a bare mountaintop, with no road. Or people talking underwater and not getting wet. It's an attention-getting device. You don't pay much attention to ordinary, commonplace images you see everyday. You get jaded.

And here is one that is strikingly contradictory, but we might have heard it so often that we don't even think of it. Robes washed clean and bright in blood. I don't know anything about lamb's blood, but I do know that it's hard to get bloodstains out of anything white.

And how about the striking contradiction that these people, who have been through great tribulation, are joyously praising and serving God in Christ?

Now, there are great catastrophes and sufferings yet to come in this book, so what really is this tribulation that the multitude has come out of?

John is writing to a church under persecution, probably that of the Emperor Domitian Caesar, who was assassinated in 97 A.D., so we are experiencing a message given around 95 or 96 A.D. John wants us to know that Christians who face the lions and the fires, whether they survive or not, will see paradise at the throne of God and the Lamb. They won't hunger or thirst, they'll have springs of living water, and God will wipe away every tear. Not that they won't have tears, but they will be comforted.

We don't face lions or fires. Yet this scripture has survived nineteen centuries to speak to us. "The Tribulation" is probably not lions or fires, but what could it mean for us? It could mean the end of time. Some believe that John is predicting a time of terrible disaster before the final reign of God. But that still doesn't fit; the multitude is before the throne prior to these later tribulations.

This tribulation might be one everyone goes through. A universal tribulation would apply to everyone, and everyone would need encouragement and comforting in the face of it. And what tribulation does everyone go through, regardless of time on this earth? Life itself. I don't mean to say that life is a terrible suffering, but everyone has hurts and sorrows and pains, what we used to call "a cross to bear." Everyone experiences the pain of life. Everyone encounters death — walking through the valley of the shadow. And everyone dies.

Now suffering by itself has no redeeming value. Pain alone wins us nothing. But when we suffer for the Word of God, as the first-century Christians did, or when we suffer anything knowing Jesus is present, we have redemption.

Notice that the multitude praising God and the Lamb are praising God and the Lamb, even after coming out of the great tribulation. Maybe the real message of Revelation is: "Praise God anyway. No matter what."

One way we can praise God right here and now is to be an encourager. When you see someone in tribulation, someone suffering from the pain and discouragement of this life, the slings and arrows of outrageous fortune, give them a word of encouragement. Sometimes just listening and understanding and having a shoulder to cry on is an encouragement.

And the thing to be careful of here is that not everyone wants encouragement, or is ready to hear or be cheered up. It might just make them mad.

Many years ago I was visiting in the home of a friend. I knew my friend to be a very faithful, courageous, and strong Christian. Well, this was just a friendly visit, and we weren't talking about much of consequence, until I had to be excused to make use of his indoor plumbing. In my friend's bathroom, taped to the mirror over the sink, was a cartoon. It showed someone holding one foot in both hands as if he had stubbed his toe, with a grimace of pain on his face. And in cheerful cartoon letters the caption read, "Praise God Anyway."

About a week later I was with this same friend and he was saying something about some trouble he was having. I happened to say, "Praise God anyway." He got a startled look on his face, and he said, "How did you know?" I just smiled. I remembered a saying I once heard, "A friend hears the song in our heart and sings it for us when we forget."

That's the kind of life God gives us. For we know that God has a warm friendly, encouraging place for us, for thousands and millions, and the number is uncounted.

Lord, help us to know the joy that is ours when we say no to everything that makes it more difficult to say yes to you.

All Things New

Years ago I worked at a telecatalog center. People called in their orders and I entered them into the computer. Each day I had to log on to my computer station with a password. It was my password. At the training session covering passwords, the trainer suggested we use something not very obvious that no one could guess. Your children's names or grandchildren. Your car license plate. Your bowling team name. In that system, the computer asked you to change your password every six weeks. So you had to think of something new you would remember, and could spell, surprisingly often.

But the main point of a password is to make it hard for anyone else to get into your system. If you've ever used a password, you'll appreciate this story.

It was Parent's Night at the high school. Mrs. Schulz walked through her son's day at high school, along with other parents. In the computer lab, her son's password didn't work. It cannot vary by even one letter or space, and some words can be deceiving. But she got an opportunity just made for mothers. The teacher helped her change the password on her son's computer. That's why young Mr. Schulz's new password is "ilovemom." (Mosley, *Emphasis*, May-June, 1998, p. 26)

One day, a teacher, a garbage collector, and a lawyer all die and go to heaven. Saint Peter is there and is having a bad day since heaven is getting crowded. When they get to the gate, Saint Peter says that there will be a test to get into heaven: they each will have to answer a single question.

To the teacher, he says, "What was the name of the ship that crashed into the iceberg and sank with over half its passengers and was the worst disaster in maritime history?"

The teacher thinks for a second, and then replies: "That would be the *Titanic*, right?" Saint Peter waves him through.

Saint Peter turns to the garbage man, and, figuring that heaven doesn't need all the stink that this guy would bring into heaven, decides to make the question a little harder: "How many people died on the ship?"

The garbage man guesses: "1,513."

"That happens to be right; go ahead."

Then Saint Peter turns to the lawyer: "Name them."

We know there will be a final judgment. And we usually think of heaven as so good that none of us is good enough to get in. We worry we won't know the password. The test questions might be too hard. So we get lots of jokes about trying to get in.

We really can't know what either heaven or hell actually is; even the Bible can't tell us because they are vast unknowns. The human mind can't grasp either one. The most we can have is what we have here in Revelation: an approximation in word-pictures that give us some idea of heaven or hell.

Today's reading from Revelation 21 gives us two ideas: 1) God is making all things new, and 2) God is preparing to dwell with his people. Let's take the second point first.

Revelation can be broken down into a play with seven acts, each act having seven scenes. Act 1 deals with the church in this world, in John's time. In Act 2 we turn to the church in heaven. And there are some bizarre pictures here, but they are not all of John's making. The four living creatures described earlier in chapter 5 come from a vision of Ezekiel, and they have elements of the vision of angels in Isaiah's vision of the temple in heaven. So John carries us back to the Old Testament for some of his imagery.

God is the God of the living, in this world and the next. And what we do here, while living in this world, shapes us for the next.

Our idea of the afterlife or heaven or hell will shape the way we shape ourselves for it. You may not be too thrilled with the picture John presents: just praise God in Christ for all eternity. But that's what he says. Could it be a picture that makes sense? It does if your life in this world tries to make every minute a practice for it: looking to Christ as central to life and his praise as its most important activity.

John says that in heaven the worship of Christ is central, comes from every living creature, and is sevenfold praise.

On the syndicated television show *The Pretender*, the hero, Jarrod, had been abducted as a child and forced to use his genius for the machinations of "The Center." Now that he's an adult and has escaped from "The Center," he sees what he missed not having a mother or family while he was growing up. He desperately wants to be reunited with his mother. He almost got to meet her once, but "The Center" got to him before he could talk to her and she had to flee the scene. Since then his thoughts have turned more and more to his mother. Along the way he helps people in trouble, but mainly he's searching for his mother.

Revelation 21 says that God's longing to be reunited with humanity is even more intense than Jarrod's longing to be reunited with his mother. That's the whole message of the Bible. In the beginning, we turned away from our Creator and God. And ever since then, God has been at work bringing us back to him. And here at the end of time, God recreates heaven and earth so that we can finally live together as one family.

Jesus' death and resurrection make it possible for us to begin to experience that family of God today. And we, as priests serving God, are to be the presence of God for others when they can't feel that presence themselves.

Remember his command, "Love one another, even as I have loved you."

God longs to be one with his people, and is preparing to dwell with them. That's why we see the Holy City, God's people the church, prepared for him as a Bride adorned for her husband.

But God is also "making all things new."

In France, September of 1783, Joseph and Jacques Montgolfier publicly demonstrated the first practical hot air balloon. Passengers on the flight were a duck, a rooster, and a sheep. Among the witnesses of the demonstration were Louis XVI and Marie Antoinette. The three animals were safely recovered, paving the way for more test flights, and human beings went up in the balloon two months later.

Also in the audience was a man invited for his reputation as an inventor and scientist. At the time, he was an ambassador from the American colonies in rebellion against England. Benjamin Franklin was in France to get help for the war effort. Looking at the Montgolfier balloon, someone asked Dr. Franklin, "But what good is it?"

Was he thinking of the nation struggling to be born across the Atlantic? Could he have known or foreseen the leap to heavier-than-air flight and the power of aviation? Might a statesman and politician of that day imagine travel to the moon and stars? Maybe not. Certainly he himself had seen the birth of many new inventions, some of them useful, some of them silly.

But what he said was, "What good is a newborn baby?" (Mosley, *Emphasis*, May-June, 1998, p. 32)

Can we be open to God doing a new thing? And not just one new thing, but making all things new?

Look at the strange story in today's Acts reading. Peter (not Paul!) is able to reach Gentiles because along with his impetuous nature he has now become able to see what God is doing beyond Peter's own limited expectations. Peter has finally learned that when you call someone "the Christ, the Son of God," you don't go on to tell him what to do (remember "get behind me, Satan"?). Nor do you deny him when it gets inconvenient. Instead you listen. You feed his sheep — and since it's his flock, you let him decide who the sheep are. When you discern the presence of the Holy Spirit, you set self aside and follow. God's loving, creative power is nothing new — it has been from before the beginning and will continue after the end (or if you prefer, in eternity which has no beginning or end). This same power is also everything new: so we can hope. We can dream great dreams. We can be encouraged and challenged to aim for that new life by loving as Jesus loves us.

This praise arises out of the joy of salvation, rather than the fear of doom. And that is precisely the hymn of the multitude in heaven: Salvation belongs to our God who sits upon the throne, and to the Lamb!

God will put new things in your life. Look for new things in your life. They may not be what you expect, or even what you want. With God, you can't be timid or afraid of new things or unknown things. Because the God who makes all things new also makes his dwelling with us. And in dwelling with us he brings all those comforting things that Revelation keeps repeating, about the wiping away the tears, and no mourning or pain, because the former things have passed away.

Lord, make of us a new thing, that your people may be prepared as your bride, saying no to everything that makes it more difficult to say yes to you.

Revelation 21:10, 22 – 22:5
Easter 6

No Temple

The long-running television medical series, *ER*, seems on the surface to be just another "reality" series — a soap opera that involves us in the lives of its characters to keep us coming back week after week. And I suppose it has to be some of that, in order to keep up its ratings and stay on television. But once in a while, a message leaks through.

At the beginning of one season, *ER*, with much hype and hoopla, had its season premier, which it did the old-fashioned way. Remember back when television started, in 1948, and for over a decade, they didn't have videotape, and most shows were done "live"? That is, the television camera broadcast just what was happening at that moment. Whatever mistakes there were, went out on the air. There were no retakes, out-takes, or bloopers that didn't get on the air. It's like a stage play, where the actors have to know all their lines and all that's going to happen, and rehearse and rehearse, and do it all the same each time.

That's life, isn't it? Life is not a test. It's an actual emergency.

Well, one fall season premiere of *ER*, Emergency Room, they did the whole one-hour show live. The set up was that a documentary camera crew was visiting the hospital to make a film and they wanted to show just what happened in the Emergency Room at that time, and also get interviews with the personnel that worked there.

There were the usual bloody accidents and in-house politics and interpersonal conflicts. But in one little incident there is a sermon worth watching the whole season for. A patient makes a mess on the floor. From behind the camera which we are looking through, we hear the cameraman ask the nurse's aide, "Do you have to clean that up?" And the aide just picks up a phone and calls housekeeping.

A little later, the janitor appears, and we see him cleaning up the mess. The cameraman interviews the janitor. "Do you think this is bad?" he says. Oh, he's seen lots worse than this. And what gets him through it? He believes in God. Oh, you could do the other jobs, doctors giving treatment, nurses carrying out orders, aides and orderlies and all, without faith. But this, cleaning up the garbage of a life, for that you have to believe in God.

And just then there is another emergency and the camera rushes away, and the cameraman says, "I'll get back to you." And the janitor says, skeptically, "Oh, I don't think you will."

Now, I am willing to say that I didn't see this janitor the rest of the season. The cameraman didn't get back to him.

Except for the last scene of the season finale. I mean the very last scene of that year. We are in a trauma treatment room and the usual crisis is taking place, with nurses calling out readings and doctors giving orders and everyone giving each other worried looks.

And the camera zooms out. It backs up through the trauma room door, and retreats down the hall and we can see activity in the other treatment rooms, but the hall is mostly deserted, except for an empty gurney or two, and ... that janitor. Mopping the hall floor. He doesn't look up, he can't, this is not the "live" episode. But it is the same janitor, who had only one speech that whole season, and it was about believing in God, and needing God for this most mundane job.

Where most sitcoms hit you over the head with their self-centeredness, *ER* is subtle about its message. So subtle you almost have to memorize the series to catch it. It's about helping others, saving lives, mending lives, giving lives. Cleaning things up. And to do it you need God. You may not see the message all the time, or even every time, or even the time they show it to you on purpose, but it's there. It doesn't have to be obvious. That's not what they are in show business for.

In Revelation, John of Patmos has a message for us. Something like that episode of *ER*, he has to be subtle to get his message out, because the Romans are censoring his mail. We don't always get his message, because John has to be obscure to stay in business.

The message from the Revelation reading today is:

1. No Temple can stand forever.
2. No Temple is God.
3. No Temple is necessary. We have God in Christ.

1. No Temple can stand forever. At the end of the first century the Christian church was struggling with its relationship to Judaism, to Rome, and the rest of the world. The Temple, the law, the sacrifice, circumcision, the Sabbath, these things made up the basic form of Judaism. The Temple was the visible sign that God was dwelling with his people. Some believed that as long as the Temple stood in Jerusalem, no enemy could destroy the city. So they could rebel against the Roman Empire and hope to survive as a nation. But they didn't. In 70 A.D., Jerusalem was sacked and the Roman Legion laid waste the Temple, leaving one wall standing.

The great vision of John the elder on the island of Patmos can be seen as a great play with seven acts. In the last act John sees the church as it will be in the end of time, and the fulfilling of the sevenfold plan of God for salvation. The old heaven and the old earth pass away. The last judgment is given. In scenes 3 and 4 of Act 7 we hear of the establishment of the New Heaven and the New Earth, and the new Jerusalem, the church. Then John describes the making of all things new, and the New Jerusalem appears again in today's lesson, to expand on the description of the church triumphant. All that's left is for John to summarize and say some things about the book itself in his epilogue.

He writes to address the rootless feeling of the time — if you reject Rome you'd better have something stronger to put in its place, especially since Jerusalem is no longer standing. He says that though the Temple no longer stands, the new Jerusalem, the church, has its entrances in Israel, with twelve gates for the twelve tribes of Israel. But its foundations are in Christianity, named for the twelve apostles of the Lamb. But this new Jerusalem has no temple, for no temple can stand for ever.

2. No Temple is God. The vision of Patmos is of Jesus the faithful witness, the firstborn of the dead, and the ruler of rulers on the earth. Further, John pictures a heaven where the worship of

Christ is central, comes from every living creature, and is seven-fold praise.

This praise arises out of the joy of salvation, rather than the fear of doom. And that is precisely the hymn of the multitude in heaven: Salvation belongs to our God who sits upon the throne, and to the Lamb!

There is a direct link between how much we praise God in this life and how much we will enjoy the next life; how much we turn to God while we are on earth reflects how prepared we are for heaven. The church's purpose is to give praise and worship to God and the Lamb. This is something we need to do wherever we are, whoever we are, no matter what we are doing. Like that janitor in the ER.

3. No Temple is necessary. We have God in Christ. God is the God of the living, in this world and the next. And what we do here, while living in this world, shapes us for the next.

The elder, or "interpreting angel," shows John a great multitude who have come out of the Great Tribulation. This tribulation might be one everyone goes through. A universal tribulation would apply to everyone, and everyone would need encouragement and comforting in the face of it. And what tribulation does everyone go through, regardless of time on this earth? Life itself. I don't mean to say that life is a terrible suffering, but everyone has hurts and sorrows and pains, what we used to call "a cross to bear." Everyone experiences the pain of life. Everyone encounters death — walking through the valley of the shadow. And everyone dies.

The multitude praising God and the Lamb are praising God and the Lamb, even after coming out of the great tribulation. Maybe the real message of Revelation is: "Praise God anyway. No matter what."

For there is a New Heaven and a New Earth, and a New Jerusalem with no temple. Because a building localizes a faith that can't be localized. It is a relationship that moves and grows and cannot be contained. It is joy and music and singing. It is believing there is a sun when the sun is not shining. It is believing in God even when he hides his presence.

Make of your life a temple of your Christian faith, a home for God and his Holy Spirit. And your life will be an act of praise.

Lord, make of us temples of your Spirit, that we may say no to whatever makes it more difficult to say yes to you.

Season Finale

I understand why people play the lottery. It's fun to daydream about the good things I could do with a big prize. I suppose it's only human to want to remove all obstacles and hardships and problems. Don't worry; be happy. But that's not the way it works. Some years ago there was a television special on lottery winners, interviewed a while after winning. The basic message was: Big money doesn't mean the end of problems; big money only means different problems. One fellow has no permanent address, moves every month, and gets his mail at a Post Office box after business hours, because of the people who are after him for his money.

Hardships and problems are just opportunities to help us understand better how the world is put together. I think that's one of the messages of the book of Revelation. In fact, it's hard to understand hardships and problems, and it's hard to understand Revelation.

I suppose the majority of Christians, if they read the Bible at all, have the most trouble with the Revelation to Saint John of the Apocalypse. If you are one of these, you are in good company. Here's an example you may remember.

There was a noted biblical scholar. A professor at a university. A pastor and a church leader. A man renowned in church history for his deep understanding of the Bible and the way he changed the church forever in the way we look at the message of scripture.

This man wrote introductions to each of the books of the Bible. Early in his life he wrote one page about the Revelation of John, saying it was so hard to understand that "it is the same as if we did not have the book at all. And there are many far better books available for us to keep." Implying that we might as well throw it out. That was early in his life before he knew what trouble was.

Later he revised his Bible introductions twice. Both times the notes about Revelation took up ten pages. The times had changed. Now he reviewed the book in detail, finding much in current events that seemed to be in fulfillment of the prophecy of John of Patmos. Now he said, "... we can profit by this book and make good use of it. First, for our comfort! We can rest assured that neither force nor lies, neither wisdom nor holiness, neither tribulation nor suffering shall suppress Christendom, but it will gain the victory and conquer at last." (Luther's Works, vol. 35, p. 409)

What made the difference? What was the change between one page of indifference and apathy to ten pages of enthusiasm and embrace? Hard times, opposition, persecution. He had been branded an outlaw, burned in effigy by mobs, chased by posses, kidnapped by friends for his own safety and exiled to live under an assumed name in disguise. But he put away his safe fortress of stone and his disguise to once again become the church leader he had been, and to find that the church of our Lord does stand victorious in the end in spite of all the world can throw against it.

He was Martin Luther. (Mosley, Emphasis, January-February, 1998, p. 16)

So if you are puzzled and troubled by Revelation, don't worry; be happy! I'd worry if you understood Revelation and were comforted by it, because that might mean you'd been through fire and persecution, hardship and trouble.

The younger Martin Luther didn't like the book of Revelation because it didn't speak of the Jesus he knew, a Jesus of Grace and Forgiveness. The older Luther knew the same Jesus, but he is a Jesus who has judgment and punishment for the wicked as well as grace and forgiveness. Jesus had not changed; Luther had changed. And this loving and forgiving man had seen many people reject love and grace and forgiveness, even church leaders and teachers of the gospel, earning only judgment and punishment for themselves.

The bottom line for Luther is: He knew Jesus. Both before and after, he knew Jesus. And he grew in that knowledge until he could see some of the side of Jesus that John of Patmos reveals in Revelation.

It's more than a coincidence that John begins his book with three titles of Jesus and ends with three I AM sayings. They bracket John's vision of the consummation of salvation history. They demonstrate John's conviction that Jesus is the centerpiece of everything that is or was or will be.

Let's look closely at these three new I AM sayings.

1. I AM coming soon. What this really means is that Jesus comes to us new every day. We have his promise in our baptism. We don't need to wait a thousand or two thousand years, and it doesn't matter what will happen at the end of time. For we have what Luther had, what John had, what the thief on the cross had. We have the assurance of Jesus that he is with us always in every age. It's like we've won the lottery.

"I am coming soon" means the same thing as we say in the Lord's Prayer, "Thy kingdom come, Thy will be done." God reigns supreme. The kingdom or reign of God is at hand, it is now, it is with us. We can feel its power when we relax our rebellion and surrender in faith and trust to the will of God.

2. Jesus also says, "I am the Alpha and the Omega, the first and the last, the beginning and the end." If I go to take a picture, I have to have a camera. Even then, I have to put film in the camera. Then I can take a picture. The film came first. The film was there when the picture was taken. The film produces a print. The film is the picture, first, last, and always. We can think of the camera as God, and the film as Jesus. If you want to stretch the analogy to its limit, the light that reflects off the object to make the picture possible can be the Holy Spirit. But the focus in Revelation is on the film.

I remember Terry Bradshaw once commenting that for some football players winning isn't everything, it's the only thing. Jesus calls himself the Alpha and the Omega. He's saying that he isn't everything, but in the life of faith, he's the only thing.

Luther makes this comment on last week's lesson from Revelation: "At last, in chapter 21, the final comfort is depicted. The holy city, fully prepared, shall be led as a bride to the eternal marriage feast. Christ alone is Lord, and all the godless are condemned and go with the devil into hell" (*Luther's Works*, Vol. 35, p. 409).

3. Jesus says, "I AM the root and offspring of David, the bright and morning star." We hear a lot about David at Christmas time: Isaiah prophesies the Messiah will come from the line of David the king, and Jesus is born in Bethlehem, the city of David. To the readers and hearers of John of Patmos, this would call to mind the warrior king who made Israel a power in world history, a conquering nation rather than the victim of a conqueror.

The morning star remains brighter longer and is the last to fade. In the heaven of Revelation, the Lord God provides the light as the Sun provides light for the earth.

John puts this saying of Jesus here to point out the assurance of Jesus that he comes from the line of King David and himself lasts to the end and is not subdued by any power other than God.

"I am coming soon; I am the Alpha and the Omega; I am the root and offspring of David, the bright and morning star."

Today's sermon is the end of this Easter series on Revelation. It's the *season finale*. But it's not a finale that just ends, with all the loose ends tied up and the questions answered and the hero gets the girl and they all live happily every after. It's more of a cliff-hanger, and just when you get the most worried, the screen flashes the words, "To Be Continued ..." and you know you have to wait until next season to find out what happens next.

But in John's vision, the end hasn't happened yet. Jesus is coming soon, but not yet. He tells us this so we can prepare for the next life in the sure and certain knowledge that God is in control. Whatever happens, we can praise God anyway!

I close with these words from Luther's Preface to Revelation: "In a word, our holiness is in heaven, where Christ is; and not in the world, before men's eyes; like goods in the marketplace. Therefore let there be offenses, divisions, heresies, and faults; let them do what they can! If only the word of the gospel remains pure among us, and we love and cherish it, we shall not doubt that Christ is with us, even when things are at their worst. As we see here in this book, that through and beyond all plagues, beasts, and evil angels Christ is nonetheless with his saints and wins the final victory" (*Luther's Works*, Vol. 35, p. 411).

Lord, help us to understand what we're supposed to understand, and even when we don't understand, to say no to everything that makes it more difficult to say yes to you.

www.ingramcontent.com/pod-product-compliance
Lightning Source LLC
Chambersburg PA
CBHW072012060426
42446CB00043B/2319